BASIC
FREEZER
RECIPES

BASIC FREEZER RECIPES

BY

PHYLLIS DEMAINE

PAPERFRONTS

**ELLIOT RIGHT WAY BOOKS
KINGSWOOD, SURREY, U.K.**

Made and Printed in Great Britain by Love & Malcomson, Ltd., Redhill, Surrey, U.K.

CONTENTS

This gives a rough outline of the contents. If you are looking for one recipe in particular, check the index.

INTRODUCTION

Every woman is something of a squirrel. If it is only the odd tin of ham we like to feel there is something 'put by'. Our ancestors salted beef and smoked fish to preserve them, now we have our Deep Freeze cabinets.

Though there are a variety of pre-frozen meals on the market it is obviously more economic to prepare one's own dishes to stock the Freezer. In *Basic Freezer Recipes*, you won't find how to cook such meals as a Mixed Grill, or how to roast a chicken. I have chosen those recipes which take time and trouble to prepare. Thus a working wife can do her cooking at weekend; a mother can be prepared for days when the children are sick, or on holiday; while the hostess will find a Freezer filled with tasty dishes a boon.

If your own favourite is not included and you are doubtful of packaging or storing details check with a recipe using similar ingredients.

BASIC FREEZING TECHNIQUE

All foods to be frozen must have some preparation. Meat from the butcher must be well wrapped in polythene sheeting or bags to exclude the air. Weighing and labelling make it easier to find the desired package later.

Vegetables must be blanched, that is, heated in boiling water before draining, cooling and packing in polythene bags. Fruits are mostly frozen in a syrup.

Home cooked meals must be allowed to cool completely before freezing, and all air excluded from the package.

An excellent guide to freezing will be found in Charlotte Trevor's Deep Freeze Secrets, a companion book in this series.

HOW TO USE THIS BOOK

The book is divided into sections; soups, fish dishes, etc.; with one recipe complete on each page. Thus there will be no need to refer to other pages. Where the length of preparation has obliged me to divide a recipe, as in the case of Hot Water Crust Pies, the method of preparing the pie case is explained on one page with the various fillings on the next.

Chain cooking is a phrase one encounters in freezing. It simply means that with bulk buying being the most economic way of stocking a freezer, many dishes can be prepared at the same time from different cuts of meat, on delivery. Similarly with a number of chickens; one could make a supply of Chicken Paprika with the joints, use the breasts for Chicken à la King, and use the frame for stock.

In the case of beef or lamb, the shin beef, minced beef, neck and breast of lamb can be made into tasty dishes before freezing. Often the cheaper cuts are frozen and then forgotten while the family enjoy the steaks and roasts.

As you will see, I recommend using one's own casseroles and dishes for storing. Beside the obvious disadvantage of the cost of purchasing quantities of waxed or foil containers there is the problem of re-heating.

Obviously waxed containers cannot be heated and one would hesitate to bring a foil container to the dining-table. If the cooked food is placed in a casserole lined with foil and then frozen, allowing about $\frac{1}{2}$ inch for expansion, it is simple to remove the dish once the food is frozen. Remember to re-parcel the foil-wrapped meal.

When required, peel off the foil and return food to original casserole. Beside the advantages mentioned before, one knows that the frozen block will fit exactly into a certain dish. It will not be the wrong shape or size which might allow it to drip over the edges on thawing; a danger if the meal is re-heated in a pre-set oven.

Note the use of less liquid content in the preparation of soups. This is to save on space required for them in the freezer.

Although I have given a rough guide to the space needed for each dish it is only when the cabinet is getting full that this matters. One might then need to decide between freezing those pies or that sack of sprouts.

Finally, don't be intimidated by the storage time given at the end of each recipe. There is not some evil spirit which will turn the stored food uneatable overnight should this date pass. A very slight deterioration in quality will ensue as the weeks go by but one would need a very fine palate to detect it. Oily fish is one exception, and also one would notice a 'shelling' of the crust of bread once the time limit is exceeded.

Wishing one's friends 'Farewell' is now out of fashion. Long ago when a family depended on what they could grow or catch, these weren't idle words. May I make a wish that with the help of your Deep Freeze and this book you may indeed 'Farewell'!

OVEN CHART

	Electric.		Gas Regulo.
	F.°	C.°	
Very slow	250-300	120-150	¼-1
Slow	300-350	150-177	2-4
Moderate	350-375	177-190	4-5
Medium Hot	375-400	190-205	5-6
Hot	400-425	205-218	6-7
Very Hot	450-500	232-316	8-10

ABBREVIATIONS

tsp: teaspoon.
tbs: tablespoon.
dsp: desertspoon.
oz: ounces.
lb: pounds.

pt: pints.
mins: minutes.
Reg: Regulo or Mark for Gas cookers.

METRIC WEIGHTS AND MEASURES

1 oz .... 28.350 grms exactly.
8 oz .... 225 grms approx.
1 lb .... 500 grms approx.
1 pt .... 500 millilitres approx.
1¾ pt .... 1 litre approx.

VEGETABLE SOUP

To make 6 portions.

Ingredients.

1 onion	2 pts stock
2 potatoes	bouquet garni
1 carrot	cornflour
¼ head of celery	seasoning.
2 tomatoes	

Peel the vegetables and dice. Put a little oil or fat into a pan and melt. Add vegetables frying for 5 min. Add stock and bouquet garni and seasoning. Simmer until vegetables are tender. Thicken slightly with cornflour. Vegetables can be passed through a fine sieve or electric blender if a creamier soup is required. Remove bouquet garni, allow to cool completely and pour into waxed containers, leaving sufficient space for liquid to expand, and freeze.

To Serve.
Reheat over a low heat. Bacon dumplings make an ideal addition to this soup. Mix 4 oz flour with 1½ oz suet and salt. Add some minced, cooked bacon or ham and mix to a firm dough with water. Form into balls and drop into simmering soup. Cook for 20 mins. till dumplings are risen and light. Alternatively, serve with fried croutons.

Storage time 2-3 months.   **Freezer space ⅛ cu ft.**

MINESTRONE SOUP

To make 8 portions.

Ingredients.

3 rashers streaky bacon
2 sticks celery
3 carrots
2 medium potatoes
1 or 2 cloves garlic
¼ tsp dried herbs
¼ small cabbage
2 tbs cornflour
1 medium onion

1 small leek
1 oz fat
1 tbs tomato purée
3 pts beef stock
1 oz spaghetti
4 oz shelled peas
2 oz grated parmesan
   cheese for serving.

Remove rind from bacon and cut into ½ inch strips. Wash, peel and slice thinly the carrots and cut potatoes into dice of ½ inch. Crush garlic. Peel and slice onion and cut leek into rings. Melt fat in saucepan add bacon, celery, carrots, potatoes, garlic, onion and leek. Fry for 5 min but do not brown. Add tomato purée, stock and herbs. Season to taste. Bring to the boil and simmer for 20 min. Wash cabbage and shred finely. Add spaghetti cut into short pieces, then peas and cabbage. Bring back to the boil and simmer for a further 20 min. Thicken with cornflour. Cook for a further 2 min. When completely cold pour into waxed cartons leaving half an inch for liquid to expand. Freeze.

To Serve.
Reheat over low heat stirring frequently. Serve with grated cheese, preferably parmesan, and chunks of fresh crusty bread.

Storage time 2-3 months.   **Freezer space ⅜ cu ft.**

SWEET CORN SOUP

To make 12 portions.

Ingredients.

2 medium onions	4 oz margarine
2 large potatoes	Cornflour
3 pts chicken stock	2 Eleven oz tins sweet corn.
½ pt milk	

Chop the onion and dice the potatoes. Fry in margarine for 5 min. Add chicken stock. Use half quantity if soup is to be frozen. Bring to the boil and simmer for 20 min. Add sweet corn and liquid and season to taste. The tins that also contain green and red peppers give this soup added colour appeal. Soup may, however, be blended if desired. Return to pan and thicken with cornflour. Allow for reduction of stock when thickening. When completely cold pour into waxed cartons leaving half an inch for liquid to expand on freezing. Freeze.

To Serve.

Reheat gently over a low heat adding more stock as required. Some of this should be milk for extra creaminess. If the soup was blended, a few dried peppers could be added for colour. Serve with triangles of crisp toast lightly buttered, or a selection of Crisp-breads. Children, especially, enjoy this soup.

Storage time 2-3 months.   **Freezer space ¼ cu ft.**

CREAM OF CUCUMBER SOUP

To make 8 portions.

Ingredients.

2 cucumbers
1½ pt chicken stock
½ pt milk

2 tbs single cream for
    serving.

Wash the cucumbers and trim off the green skin if badly marked. Cut into thick slices and then quarters. Place in saucepan with chicken stock. Bring to the boil and simmer for 5 min. If possible blend until creamy. Alternatively pass through a fine sieve. Return to pan and add milk. Bring back to the boil and season to taste. When completely cold pour into waxed cartons allowing ½ inch for expansion. Freeze.

To Serve.
Reheat slowly over low heat. Put a little cream on each portion and serve piping hot.

Storage time 2-3 months.   **Freezer space ⅛ cu ft.**

SPINACH SOUP

To make 4 portions.

Ingredients.

1 pt chicken stock
4½ oz. frozen spinach

1 egg.

Put stock and spinach into pan and boil. Simmer for 5 min. Add a little soup to the beaten egg and mix. Return to pan and stir until soup thickens. When cold pour into cartons, allowing space for expansion, and freeze. This is an ideal slimmer's recipe.

To Serve.
Reheat slowly stirring often. Do not boil.

Storage time 2 months.   **Freezer space minimal,**

HAM AND PEA SOUP

To make 12 portions

Ingredients.
1½ pt chicken stock   ½ pt milk
2 lb garden peas   seasoning.
4 slices cooked ham

Add peas to chicken stock which is already boiling. Cut up the ham and put some aside if some soup is to be served directly. Add to the stock and simmer for 5 min. If blender available, blend soup, otherwise mince ham before adding. Return to the pan and bring back to the boil. Add milk and season to taste. Simmer for a further 5 min. Pour that soup which is to be eaten into soup cups and sprinkle a little ham over the top. Allow the rest to cool completely and pour into waxed cartons and freeze. Remember to leave ½ inch for liquid to expand on freezing.

To Serve.
Turn soup into saucepan and reheat over a low heat. The addition of Parsley Dumplings make this soup much more satisfying.

Dumplings. Mix 4 oz flour with 1½ oz shredded suet and ¼ tsp salt and 1 tsp chopped parsley. Mix to a firm dough with water. Form into balls and drop into hot soup. Cook for 15-20 min until dumplings are light and fluffy.

Storage time 2 months.   **Freezer space ⅛ cu ft.**

KIDNEY SOUP

To make 8 portions.

Ingredients.

2 medium onions	½ pt milk
8 lamb kidneys	seasoning
2 oz margarine	a little cream for serving
2 pt water	chopped parsley for
1 desertspoon cornflour	serving.

Peel and chop the onions. Remove skin and core from kidneys and cut into small pieces. Melt margarine in saucepan and allow to cook for 2 min. Add the kidneys and cook for 4 min. Add water (quantity can be halved to save freezer space). Cover and bring to the boil. Simmer for 10 min. Thicken with cornflour. This soup may be 'blended' if desired but it is not necessary. When completely cold pour into waxed cartons leaving ½ inch for expansion and freeze.

To Serve.

Turn soup into a saucepan and reheat over a low heat. If stock has been reduced add more at this stage. For a much richer looking soup it may be coloured with a little gravy browning. Add milk in proportion to soup being reheated. Drip a spoonful of cream on to each portion and a scattering of chopped parsley.

Without the extra stock and perhaps a little more thickening this soup could be served with creamed potatoes.

Storage time 3 months.   **Freezer space ⅛ cu ft.**

TOMATO AND CELERY SOUP

To make 6 portions.

Ingredients.

1 lb tomatoes	$\frac{3}{4}$ pt chicken stock
1 large potato	$\frac{1}{2}$ pt milk for serving.
2 sticks celery	

Wash and cut the tomatoes into quarters removing hard core. Scrape and slice thinly the potato. Wash and chop celery. Place the vegetables in a large saucepan with the chicken stock. Cover and bring to the boil. Simmer for 20 min. Blending soups in an electric blender improves the texture of most soups but a satisfactory result can be obtained by passing the ingredients through a fine sieve. Return to pan and bring to the boil again. Season to taste. When completely cold pack into waxed cartons leaving $\frac{1}{2}$ inch for expansion, and freeze.

To Serve.

Turn soup into saucepan and reheat over a low heat. Add milk and allow to just reach boiling point. Serve with croutons. Fry thin cubes of bread until golden brown and crisp in hot fat. Float on top of each portion. If this soup is to be made in greater quantities the amount of stock can be halved to conserve freezer space. Remember to add stock to the correct amount when reheating.

Storage time 2-3 months.   **Freezer space minimal.**

ASPARAGUS SOUP

To make 6 portions.

Ingredients.

10½ oz can Asparagus tips   3½ oz single cream for
1½ pt chicken stock   serving.
Cornflour to thicken
seasoning

An easily made soup which can be made in sufficient
quantities to eat and freeze as desired. The above amounts
can be doubled or trebled. Stir the Asparagus tips and
the liquid into the chicken stock and bring to the boil
stirring continually. Cover and simmer for 20 min. Pass
through a fine sieve or blend if electric blender available.
Return to pan. Season to taste and thicken with the cornflour. The soup is now ready for eating with the addition
of a little cream on top of each portion. For storing allow
to cool completely and pack into waxed cartons leaving
half an inch for liquid to expand. Freeze.

To Serve.

Reheat over a low heat. As this makes an ideal soup for
entertaining it can be heated when most convenient and
poured into a large vacuum flask to be decanted when
required. Drip a whirl of cream into each soup cup to lie
on each portion. Most soups will keep hot in a flask for
convenience in serving with no change in their flavour.

Storage time 2-3 months.   **Freezer space ⅛ cu ft.**

BROWN ONION SOUP

To make 12 portions.

Ingredients.

1 lb small onions	**4 pt beef stock**
2 oz margarine	**seasoning.**

Peel and slice onions and fry for 3-4 min in margarine until golden brown, using a saucepan. Add stock and season, using only half stock to conserve space in freezer. Bring to the boil and simmer for 15 min. When completely cold pour into waxed cartons and freeze leaving half an inch for expansion.

To Serve.

Reheat over a low heat. Serve with:

SAVOURY ENVELOPES

Ingredients.

8 oz plain flour	**water.**
1 tsp salt	
4 oz mixed margarine and lard	

Filling

4 oz cold cooked minced meat.	**2 tbs vegetable soup.**

Rub fat into flour until mixture resembles fine breadcrumbs. Add salt and mix to a firm dough with water. Make filling. Mix meat with vegetable soup. Roll out the pastry thinly and cut into 3½ in. rounds. Place a heaped spoonful of the meat on each piece and damp edges. Fold over, seal edges and flute. Freeze on baking trays to keep separated. Store in polythene bags.

To Serve.

Fry envelopes in deep fat until pale golden brown. Add to soup on serving. Can be used with various other soups.

Storage time 3 months.   **Freezer space ⅛ cu ft.**

LEEK AND POTATO SOUP

To make 12 portions.

Ingredients.

2 lb potatoes	4 oz margarine
2 lb leeks	2 pt chicken stock
2 onions	seasoning.
1 pt milk	

Peel and dice the potatoes. Wash and slice the leeks. Peel and slice onions. Melt the margarine in a saucepan and put in the vegetables. Cook gently, tossing to coat vegetables in fat, for approximately 5 min. Season and add stock. Bring to the boil and cover. Simmer for 20 min. Blend, in small quantities in an electric blender, or pass through a fine sieve. Return to pan and add milk. Bring to the boil. Allow to cool and then pack in waxed cartons. Allow $\frac{1}{2}$ inch for expansion. Freeze.

To Serve.

Return to the saucepan and reheat over a low heat. Do not boil briskly. Serve with croutons. Cut thin bread into cubes and fry in hot fat until golden and crisp. With this soup brown or wholemeal bread would be ideal. If no croutons are available serve with Crisp-breads lightly buttered. A dash of garlic pepper over each portion gives this soup that something extra.

Croutons can be made with stale bread and stored in polythene bags in the freezer for use with most soups.

Storage time 2-3 months.   **Freezer space $\frac{1}{8}$ cu ft.**

BEEF AND BEAN BROTH

To make 12 portions.

Ingredients.

2 large onions	8 oz corned beef
2 medium carrots	2 8 oz tins baked beans
2 sticks celery	3 pt stock.

Chop the onions and fry in oil. Dice carrots and cut celery into small slices. Add to the onions and fry together with corned beef for 5 min. Add baked beans and stock, using only half quantity if wishing to conserve freezer space. Diced potatoes may be added in the same quantity as carrots. Bring to the boil and simmer for 20 min. When broth is completely cold pour into waxed cartons leaving half an inch for liquid to expand, and freeze.

To Serve.

Return sufficient broth to saucepan and add stock if required. Heat slowly until broth boils and serve piping hot. Omitting the extra stock this can also make an excellent pie filling. Turn into a deep oven-proof dish and make a crust by rubbing 3 oz fat into 6 oz flour with a pinch of salt. Mix to a firm dough with water and roll out to fit dish. Put into a cold oven set for 375° Reg 5 and bake until crust is a golden brown.

Storage time 2-3 months.   **Freezer space ¼ cu ft.**

QUICK BROTH

To make 16 portions.

Ingredients.

4 oz fat	1 oz cornflour
2 onions	4 pt meat stock
4 carrots	2 tbs oil
2 small parsnips	8 oz. mushrooms
4 sticks celery	seasoning
8 oz cooked meat	mixed herbs.

Wash vegetables and chop onions finely. The carrots, parsnips and celery should be diced. Toss all the vegetables in pan, in melted fat, over medium heat. Pour in stock, stirring, and bring to the boil. Sprinkle in the herbs and simmer for 30 min. stirring occasionally. Meanwhile chop mushrooms and fry in oil. Dice the meat and add this and the mushrooms to the soup. Bring back to the boil and simmer a further 5 min. Thicken if desired with cornflour. When completely cold pour into waxed cartons and freeze. Half quantity of stock can be used if all the broth is to be frozen but do not fill cartons, allow ½ inch for expansion.

To Serve.

Return desired quantity of broth to a saucepan adding more stock as required. Heat over a moderate heat bringing to the boil and allowing to simmer till vegetables are heated through. Serve in deep bowls with chunks of bread cut from a French Stick.

Storage time 2-3 months.   **Freezer space ⅓ cu ft.**

PLAIN AND PIQUANT MUSHROOM SOUP

To make 12 portions.

Ingredients.

4 oz butter	1 lb mushrooms
2 pt chicken stock	seasoning
1 pt milk	1 oz cornflour.

Additions for Piquant Soup.

4 tbs chopped parsley	$\frac{1}{4}$ pt cream for serving.
juice of 2 lemons	

There is no necessity to use best quality mushrooms for either of these soups, stalks or over-large mushrooms will do just as well. Chop the mushrooms finely and fry in butter. Add chicken stock and milk and seasoning. Bring to the boil and simmer for 20 min. Thicken with cornflour. Cool, and pack in waxed cartons leaving $\frac{1}{2}$ inch for liquid to expand. Freeze. A quantity can be frozen in ice-cube trays to provide stock cubes. For Piquant Soup add the chopped parsley and lemon juice before simmering. This makes an ideal soup when entertaining.

To Serve.

Return soup to a saucepan and reheat over a low heat. In the case of the Piquant Soup add a spoonful of cream to each portion on serving. Either of these soups can be thickened and used as a tasty sauce with roast chicken. Or, pieces of chicken meat can be reheated in the sauce for a quick snack; serve with crisp-breads.

Storage time 2 months. **Freezer space $\frac{1}{8}$ cu ft.**

TOMATO SOUP

To make 8 portions.

Ingredients.

2 rashers bacon	2 pt stock
½ onion	bouquet garni
1 lb tomatoes	1 carrot.

Cut the rind off the bacon and cut bacon into small pieces. Chop onion and dice carrot. Cut up tomatoes. Fry the vegetables in a little oil and add the stock. Bring to the boil and season to taste. Add bouquet garni and cover. Simmer for approximately 45 min. Put vegetables through a fine sieve or electric blender. Return to pan and thicken with cornflour. When completely cold remove bouquet garni, pour into waxed containers and freeze. Remember to leave ½ inch for expansion.

To Serve.

Return to pan and heat gently over low heat. Add a little cream or 'top of the milk' to each portion just before serving. If liked, noodles can be added to soup before it is completely heated. Allow noodles to cook for 15 min. The noodles can either be bought ready-made or made at home.

Noodles. Rub 1 oz fat into ½ lb seasoned flour, mix stiffly with an egg and a little water. Roll out thinly and cut into noodles. Leave to stand for ½ hr in floured cloth.

Storage time 3 months.　　　　　　　**Freezer space ⅛ cu ft.**

TOMATO PURÉE

To make 1 pt of purée.

Ingredients.

2 lb tomatoes	¼ tsp powdered basil leaves
1 small onion	seasoning
1 bay leaf	1 tsp sugar.

Skin the tomatoes by covering with boiling water. Chop and core fruit and place in pan with chopped onion and herbs. Heat slowly until there is sufficient juice to prevent burning then bring to the boil and simmer until onion is soft. Pass mixture through a fine sieve. Return to pan and continue to simmer until mixture is thicker. Season to taste with salt, pepper and sugar and leave to cool. Spoon into small containers leaving room for expansion. Freeze.

To Serve.

Allow a container of purée to thaw in the fridge. Use in soups, stews and pasta dishes as recipe dictates. Always store residue in the fridge. Many recipes in this book call for tomato purée and although the commercial product is excellent it can be more economical to prepare a stock when tomatoes are cheap. If the fruit is not very firm this will not deter from the finished purée.

Storage time 6 months. **Freezer space minimal.**

FISH AU GRATIN

To make 4 portions.

Ingredients.

1 lb white fish	cornflour
1 pt milk	seasoning.
3 oz cheese	

Skin fish if necessary and put to cook in a little milk to which a knob of butter and salt and pepper have been added. When fish begins to flake, remove from pan and put into a foil-lined casserole to cool. Add the pint of milk and bring to the boil. Grate the cheese and add to the milk. Thicken the sauce with cornflour and allow to cool. Pour over the fish. A topping of creamed potatoes can be added and the whole put into a polythene bag to freeze. The casserole may be removed when food is frozen. Return food to bag.

To Serve.

Remove foil and return food to original casserole. Reheat in moderate oven 350° Reg 4 for 1½ hr. Remove lid and dot with margarine to brown potatoes for last 15 min. If the Fish Au Gratin has been frozen alone it can be reheated gently in a saucepan. Creamed potatoes and a colourful vegetable should be served with it. Sweetcorn makes an ideal garnish.

Storage time 3 months.   **Freezer space ⅛ cu ft.**

COD PROVENCALE

To make 3 family size or 12 individual portions.

Ingredients.

1 oz seasoned flour
oil for frying
3 small onions
1 clove garlic

2 large tins tomatoes
3 lb skinned cod
1 tsp oregano
seasoning.

Slice onions and crush garlic. Cut fish into 12 portions and dip in seasoned flour. Fry in the oil until golden brown on both sides, approximately 8 min. Drain and put into three family sized foil lined casseroles. Pack individual portions in rigid foil containers if desired. Fry onion and garlic in remaining oil in pan. Pour in the tomatoes, breaking the fruit with a fork. Sprinkle in the oregano. Toss over a brisk heat for 2 to 3 min. Add seasoning to taste. Allow to cool and pour over fish. Cool before putting casseroles into polythene bags to freeze. Fasten mouth with wire twisters. When frozen, remove dishes and replace food in bags.

To Serve.
Remove foil while frozen and put fish into casserole with lid. Reheat in a moderate oven 350° Reg 4 for 1½ hr. Serve with creamed potatoes.
The individual portions could be topped with a layer of creamed potato before freezing thus ensuring a complete meal in one pack. If frozen in foil dishes they can be reheated in the oven, removing lid to brown potato.

Storage time 4 months.   **Freezer space ½ cu ft.**

FISHERMAN'S STEW

To make 4 portions.

Ingredients.

1 lb cod	1 pt white sauce
4 oz prawns	small quantity shrimp paste
4 scallops	2 oz margarine
12 oz leeks	seasoning.
8 oz potatoes	

Wash leeks and cut into ¼ inch slices. Dice potatoes. Fry leeks and potatoes in a little margarine without browning. Place cod in casserole along with the peeled prawns. Cut scallops into four pieces and toss in melted butter. Add to casserole. Drain surplus fat from potatoes and leeks and pour vegetables over fish. Make a white sauce from 1 pt milk, seasoned, and thickened with cornflour. Flavour with shrimp paste. Cook in moderate oven 350° Reg 4 for 30 min. When completely cold put into foil lined casserole and freeze. Casserole dish may be removed when fish is frozen. Return fish to polythene bag.

To Serve.

Remove foil and return to original casserole. Reheat in a moderate oven 350° Reg 4, placing dish in oven while it is still cold, unless food has been allowed to thaw. Allow approximately 1 hr, for heating through. Make large croutons by frying triangles of bread in margarine or bacon fat until golden brown. Or serve with crisp toast.

Storage time 2 months.   **Freezer space ⅛ cu ft.**

CURRIED COD

To make 8 portions.

Ingredients.

8 thick cod steaks
juice of 1 lemon
1 tbs cornflour
2 pts chicken stock

2 tbs curry powder
2 tbs tomato purée
1 large onion.

Blend the cornflour with tomato purée and curry powder. Chop onion and stir into mixture. Slowly add chicken stock and season to taste. Put cod steaks into saucepan and sprinkle with lemon juice. Pour the sauce over fish. Cover and simmer for 10 mins. When completely cold put into suitable sized containers or foil lined casseroles. Freeze. Remove dishes, if required, when food is frozen.

To Serve.
Remove foil if used, and turn into a saucepan and reheat over a low heat. Alternatively, put into a moderate oven 350° Reg 4 for 1 hr. Serve with boiled rice. Boil 2 oz rice per person in plenty of salted water for 15 min. Drain into a colander and rinse with hot water to separate grains. A little saffron can be added for the last 5 min cooking time if liked, adding a little more colour to the dish.

Storage time 2 months.   **Freezer space ¼ cu ft.**

STUFFED PLAICE

To make 4 portions.

Ingredients.
1½ lb plaice fillets
2 oz bread crumbs
½ level tsp marjoram
1 tsp parsley
grated rind ½ lemon.
5 tbs milk

Sauce.
1 pt milk and water
cornflour
2 tbs mayonnaise
seasoning.

Put the breadcrumbs, herbs and lemon rind into a bowl, season and mix well. Stir in the 5 tbs of milk. Wash and dry the fillets of plaice. Spread the stuffing on to the fish. Grease a large piece of foil with butter and make up a parcel of the fish and stuffing in the foil. Alternatively wrap individually. Place in polythene bags and freeze.

To Serve.
Place parcels of fish on to a baking sheet, checking that there are no tears in the foil wrappings. Bake slowly at 300° Reg 2 for 1 hr. Make a white sauce with the milk and seasoning and thicken with cornflour. Stir in the mayonnaise. When fish is cooked remove from foil, unwrapping carefully to conserve juices, and serve with the sauce. Serve with spinach or garden peas. It would be as lengthy to reheat if fish were already cooked. This way the preparation can be done when it is convenient.

Storage time 4 months.   **Freezer space ⅛ cu ft.**

POLISH SOLE

To make 8 portions.

Ingredients.

2 lb sole	**flour**
4 tbs parmesan cheese	**breadcrumbs**
¼ pt sour cream	**butter.**

Cover fish with seasoned flour and fry in butter to brown slightly. Arrange in a casserole and sprinkle liberally with parmesan cheese. Pour over the sour cream. Sprinkle breadcrumbs over and dot with knobs of butter. Bake in a moderately hot oven 400° Reg 6 for 20 min. When completely cold spoon into a waxed container and freeze.

To Serve.
Turn into a saucepan and heat gently over low heat. Thicken sauce with a little cornflour. Alternatively heat in a casserole in the oven for approximately 30 min. Serve with baked or creamed potatoes and a vegetable. Sweetcorn or cauliflower or broccoli are ideal with this dish. If the flavour of parmesan cheese proves too strong for your palate, any other cheese can be substituted, but the distinctive Polish taste is then lost.
Other white fish can be enhanced by cooking in sour cream in this way.
Garnish with lemon slices.

Storage time 2 months.   **Freezer space ⅛ cu ft.**

COD IN CIDER

To make 8 portions.

Ingredients.

8 pieces cod	1 small red pepper
2 large onions	large tin tomatoes
2 lemons	½ pt cider
2 or 3 mushrooms	1 tbs cooked peas.

Slice onions and put into pan with a little water. Bring to the boil and drain off water. Grate lemon rind finely and mix into onions. Chop the lemon flesh and stir into onions. Add the mushrooms and pepper. Break up tomatoes and add, along with a little parsley, if liked. Grease a casserole and spread half the onion mixture in bottom. Lay the fish on top and cover with rest of onion mixture. Season well, and pour the cider over. Cover with buttered paper and bake in moderate oven 350° Reg 4 for 45-60 min. When completely cold spoon into waxed container and freeze.

To Serve.
Turn into a pan and heat gently over low heat or put into a casserole and heat through in the oven. Add peas for the last few minutes and sprinkle with parsley before serving. White wine can be used in place of cider.

Storage time 2 months. **Freezer space ⅛ cu ft.**

FISH CASSEROLE

To make 6 portions.

Ingredients.

1 lb fish fillets	¾ pt milk
6 medium potatoes	1 egg
2 carrots	1 tbs breadcrumbs
1 onion	1 oz butter
1 bay leaf	salt.

Slice potatoes and carrots and chop onion. Cut fish into small pieces. Grease a casserole dish with butter and put the fish and vegetables in layers into the dish. Sprinkle with salt and lay bay leaf on top. Beat egg and milk and pour over the fish and vegetables. They should only barely be covered. Sprinkle over the breadcrumbs and dot with butter. Cover and bake in a moderate oven 350° Reg 4 for approximately 50 min until vegetables are tender. When completely cold pour into waxed container or foil-lined casserole and freeze. Casserole may be removed on freezing. Return food to polythene bag.

To Serve.

Remove foil, if used, and return food to original casserole. Reheat in moderate oven for 1 hr. Or heat over low heat in a saucepan, stirring occasionally. Remove bay leaf before freezing. Serve direct from dish. A green vegetable may be served also to add more colour. Tinned sweetcorn makes an ideal accompaniment to any fish dish.

Storage time 2 months.   **Freezer space ⅛ cu ft.**

B

FISH THERMIDOR

To make 4 portions.

Ingredients.

1 lb fish fillets:	1 cup grated cheese
cod, halibut, etc.	dash of paprika
¼ cup sherry	cornflour
1 onion	1 cup chicken stock.
4 ozs mushrooms	

Place fish in casserole. Slice mushrooms and fry in oil. Spoon them over the fish. Chop onion and mix with stock, sherry, and seasoning, in a pan and bring to the boil. Thicken with cornflour and add cheese, stirring until cheese melts. Pour over fish, cover and bake for ½ hr, in moderate oven 350° Reg 4. When completely cold, spoon into waxed container or foil lined casserole and freeze.

To Serve.

Remove foil if used and return to casserole. Heat in moderate oven for 1 hr. Or turn into a pan and heat over low heat. Before serving sprinkle with paprika. Serve with creamed potatoes. Or pipe potatoes on to a greased baking sheet and brown alongside the fish. Potatoes baked in their jackets suit this dish also. Spinach or other colourful vegetables are ideal with this dish as it lacks colour (apart from the paprika).

Storage time 4 months.   **Freezer space ⅛ cu ft.**

SOLE BONNE FEMME

To make 4 portions.

Ingredients.

4 large fillets of sole	3 oz mushrooms
$\frac{1}{4}$ pt white wine	1 oz butter.
$\frac{1}{4}$ pt white sauce	

Place the fillets of sole into a casserole and sprinkle with salt and a little parsley if liked. Pour the white wine over and cover the dish with buttered paper. Bake in a moderate oven 350° Reg 4 for 15 min until fish is just tender. Meanwhile make the white sauce by bringing $\frac{1}{4}$ pt seasoned milk to the boil and thickening with cornflour. Slice the mushrooms and fry in butter and add to the sauce. Drain the wine off the fish into the sauce and stir over a low heat briskly until smooth. Put the fish into a foil lined casserole when cold and pour over the sauce. Place casserole into a polythene bag and freeze. Remove dish when frozen and return fish to bag.

To Serve.

Remove foil and return fish to casserole. Heat in moderate oven until fish is hot. Stir sauce gently, occasionally, to ensure a smooth creamy finish. Serve on a hot dish surrounded with a ring of piped, creamed potatoes. Garnish with parsley sprigs and lemon slices.

Storage time 3 months.   **Freezer space $\frac{1}{8}$ cu ft.**

TUNA AND CHEESE MOUSSE

To make one 2 pt Mousse.

Ingredients.

1 lb cottage or soft cheese	watercress
7 oz can tuna fish	½ oz gelatine
5 oz yogurt	¼ pt water.
juice ½ lemon	

Put the water and gelatine in a basin and melt over a pan of hot water. Mix the tuna fish, yogurt, cheese and lemon juice together. Chop the watercress leaves leaving a few for garnish and add to the cheese and fish mixture. Stir in the dissolved gelatine and mix well. Pour into a 2 pt soufflé dish and leave to cool and set. Garnish with watercress leaves if serving. If freezing set in waxed or foil container and freeze.

To Serve.

Allow mousse to thaw to room temperature and add garnish of watercress leaves. Serve with crisp, hot, buttered toast and tomato salad. Other tinned fish such as salmon or sardines could be used in place of the tuna fish. If fresh fish is used then a strongly flavoured one must be chosen. The addition of chopped shrimps or even shrimp paste would enhance the colour and taste.

Storage time 2-3 months.   **Freezer space ⅛ cu ft.**

CHICKEN PAPRIKA

To make 12 portions.

Ingredients.

2 onions chopped	2 large tbs paprika
oil to fry	½ pt white wine
2 tbs tomato purée	2 tbs flour
2 sliced green peppers	2 tbs lemon juice
12 chicken joints	8 tbs single cream.
seasoning	

Fry the onions in the oil until golden brown. Add sliced peppers and continue to fry. Sprinkle in the paprika. Put in the chicken joints, season and fry gently, turning to brown, for approximately 15 min. Pour in the wine. Cover and simmer until chicken is tender. Take out joints and divide between foil containers or foil lined dishes. Stirring sauce, add flour and when thoroughly mixed add purée. Bring to boil then reduce heat. Add lemon to single cream (top of the milk will do) and stir into sauce. Pour sauce over chicken and allow to cool. Cover containers with lids and freeze. If casserole dishes are used, remove after freezing, returning food to the polythene bags in which the dishes were originally put to freeze.

To Serve.

Reheat in a slow oven 300° Reg 2 for 1½ hr Or allow to thaw and heat in a covered pan. Serve with creamed potatoes and green vegetables. Tinned celery hearts or frozen green beans are excellent.

Storage time 2 months. **Freezer space ¾ cu ft.**

CHICKEN DE-MAINE

To make 4 portions.

Ingredients.

4 chicken joints	1 pt stock
6 oz mushrooms	¼ pt white wine
1 onion	oil for frying.

The joints from an already roasted chicken may be used for this quick, tasty dish. Flour joints and sauté in hot oil. Push to one side and fry chopped onion and mushrooms in the same oil. Pour on the wine and bring to the boil, cooking rapidly for 2 min. Any white wine will do especially the home brewed variety.* Add stock and simmer for 10 min to heat chicken through. Thicken sauce with corn-flour if necessary. Allow to cool completely before freezing.

To Serve.

Turn into a pan and reheat over a gentle heat. Serve with creamed potatoes or rice. Boil 2oz of long grain rice per person in well salted water for approximately 15 min. Drain in a colander and rinse with cold water to separate the grains. Sweetcorn makes an ideal vegetable to serve with this dish. It is possible to buy large catering tins of corn. Divide into small containers and freeze, to be gently heated when required. Alternatively serve with french beans.

Storage time 3 months.   **Freezer space ⅛ cu ft.**

---

* See "Easymade Wine and Country Drinks", uniform with this book.

COQ AU VIN

To make 8 portions.

Ingredients.

8 chicken portions	½ bottle red wine
butter to fry	24 small onions
oil to fry	1 pt chicken stock
2 cloves garlic (optional)	bouquet garni
8 oz mushrooms	cornflour.
4 tbs cognac	

Dip chicken portions in flour and fry in mixture of butter and oil. Turn until golden brown all over. Some cubes of bacon can be fried in the same oil if desired. Crush the garlic cloves and add with the mushrooms and tiny onions. Pour the cognac into a hot ladle and ignite. While flaming pour over the chicken. Shake the pan gently until flames die down. Add the stock made from stock cubes and the chicken giblets. Put in bouquet garni and bring to the boil, boiling fiercely to reduce amount of stock. Remove bouquet garni and add the red wine. Cover and simmer for approximately 1 hr. Remove the chicken and divide over suitable containers. Thicken sauce with cornflour and pour over chicken. Allow to cool and freeze.

To Serve.
Reheat and serve with fried croutons and potatoes.

Storage time 2 months.   **Freezer space ⅛ cu ft.**

CHICKEN A LA KING

To make 3 family size or 12 individual portions.

Ingredients.

oil to fry
1½ lb mushrooms
2 oz cornflour
2 pt chicken stock
seasoning

3 cups single cream
12 cups small pieces of
   cooked chicken
6 pimentos
1 cup dry sherry.

Slice the mushrooms and fry for 5 min. Blend in the corn-flour and seasoning. Slowly add stock, cream and sherry, (top of the milk may be used) stirring until sauce boils. Cook gently over low heat for 5 min. Divide the chicken and pimentos over three foil lined casserole dishes or 12 individual foil containers. When the sauce is cool pour over the chicken. Place lids on small containers but put the casseroles into polythene bags. Fasten mouths with wire twisters. Dishes may be removed for further use once food is frozen. Return foil parcels to bag and secure.

To Serve.
Reheat in warm oven 350° Reg 4 for 1½ hr. Serve with creamed potatoes and green vegetables. The individual packs make an ideal meal-for-one served with crisp toast. When several chickens are bought and the joints made into other dishes this is an excellent recipe to use the other parts. The carcasses can then be boiled for stock and sub-sequently used in the preparation of soups.

Storage time 2 months.   **Freezer space ½ cu ft.**

COLOMBO CHICKEN

To make 4 portions.

Ingredients.

oil for frying	1 pt chicken stock
1 onion	1 tsp tomato ketchup
4 chicken joints	cornflour
1 tbs curry powder	2 bananas for serving.

Chop onion and fry in oil for 5 min. Add chicken joints and brown. Remove joints from pan. Stir in curry powder and cook for 3 min. Add stock and tomato ketchup. Bring to the boil and season to taste. Return chicken to pan cover and simmer for 30 min. Thicken with cornflour. If dish is to be eaten directly peel bananas and cut in half lengthways. Place chicken on warm serving dish and heat bananas through in the sauce. Spoon sauce and bananas over chicken. Do not attempt to freeze bananas, but allow chicken and curry sauce to cool completely and put into waxed containers. Freeze.

To Serve.
Turn into a saucepan and heat through. Remove chicken and put on warm serving dish. Peel and slice bananas and heat in sauce. Spoon over chicken. Serve with rice. Allow 2 oz rice per person and boil in plenty of salted water. Rinse with hot water to separate grains.

Storage time 3 months.   **Freezer space $\frac{1}{8}$ cu ft.**

CANTONESE CHICKEN

To make 4 portions.

Ingredients.

4 chicken joints	½ pt chicken stock
2 tbs cooking oil	garlic salt and pepper
8 oz tin bean sprouts	1 tsp powdered ginger
2 oz mushrooms	1 tbs soy sauce
1 green pepper	2 tbs red wine.

Put powdered ginger, garlic salt and pepper into a polythene bag. Put in joints and toss in seasoning. Fry seasoned joints in oil until lightly browned. Remove chicken into a casserole and fry mushrooms and green pepper, sliced, in remaining oil. Add to chicken and stir in the bean sprouts. Bring chicken stock to the boil and thicken with cornflour. Stir in soy sauce and wine and pour over chicken. Cook in moderate oven 350° Reg 4 for 1½ hr. Turn into foil lined casserole or waxed container and freeze. If casserole is required remove when frozen and return food to polythene bag.

To Serve.

Remove foil if used and return to casserole. Heat in moderate oven for 1 hr. Or heat over gentle heat in a saucepan. Serve with boiled rice. Allow 2 oz rice per person and boil in plenty of salted water for 15 min. Drain and rinse with hot water to separate grains. Remember to check seasoning as some flavour is lost on freezing.

Storage time 3 months.　　　　**Freezer space ⅛ cu ft.**

BRAISED PEACHES WITH CHICKEN

To make 6 portions.

Ingredients.

1 chicken cut into 6 pieces	15 oz tin peach halves
3 rashers bacon	½ lb frozen peas
1 small onion	chicken stock
seasoning	cornflour.
oil to fry	

Remove rind from bacon and cut into thin strips. Slice the onion. Fry chicken joints and bacon and onion in hot oil until chicken browns. Transfer to casserole. Strain syrup from peaches and make up into ½ pt with chicken stock or water. Pour liquid over chicken, cover and cook in hot oven 400° Reg 6 for 30 mins. Add the peas and cook a further 15 min. Add peach halves and leave for another 5 min reducing heat to 300° Reg 2. When completely cold divide between foil lined casseroles or individual containers and freeze. Casseroles may be removed on freezing.

To Serve.

Remove foil and return to original casseroles or reheat in containers if heat proof. Place in cold oven set to reach 350° Reg 4 and cook for 1 hr, timed from reaching correct temperature. Thicken gravy with a little cornflour mixed to a paste with water. Serve with boiled rice. Allow 2 oz per person and boil in plenty of well salted water for 15 min. Drain into colander and rinse with hot water. Ideal recipe for chain cooking.

Storage time 3 months.   **Freezer space ¼ cu ft.**

CHICKEN AND HAM LOAF

To make 1 loaf.

Ingredients.

8 oz cooked chicken	1 tsp made mustard
8 oz cooked ham	few drops Worcester sauce
3 oz white bread	seasoning
2 eggs	parsley.

Line a 1 lb loaf tin with foil. Mince the chicken and ham and bread (weighed without crusts). Mix meat, breadcrumbs and parsley together in a large bowl. Add the mustard and Worcester sauce and season to taste. Stir in the well beaten eggs and mix altogether thoroughly. Press mixture into the loaf tin. Cover with foil and bake for 30 min in moderate oven 350° Reg 4. When firm to touch take out of oven and leave to cool in the tin. When sufficient time has elapsed for the loaf to be cold right through put tin into a polythene bag and freeze. The tin can be removed when loaf is frozen and the loaf returned to bag.

To Serve.

Remove foil while loaf is still frozen and allow to thaw to room temperature, approximately 4 hr. But slicing will be neater and easier if done before thawing is complete. Serve slices with a salad. It is ideal to take on picnics as it is much more moist than sliced meat. The loaf also makes an ideal sandwich filling. These quantities can be increased and the mixture of meats varied.

Storage time 1 month.   **Freezer space ⅛ cu ft.**

MEDITERRANEAN CHICKEN

To make 8 portions.

Ingredients.

2 small onions	8 chicken joints
8 rashers bacon	3 pts boiling water
4 oz mushrooms	2 tsp salt
4 oz margarine	1 tsp tumeric
16 oz rice	2 tbs parsley.

Slice the onions and remove rind from bacon. Cut bacon into 2 inch strips. Wash mushrooms. Melt margarine in bottom of grill pan after taking out the grid. Dip chicken joints in fat to coat and then put aside. Add onion, bacon and mushrooms. Toss them in margarine and lay joints on top. Grill for 30-35 min turning once and stirring the onion and bacon mixture. The joints must be crisp, golden brown and cooked through. Put boiling water with salt and tumeric into pan and add rice. Cook for 15 min until tender. Drain rice into colander and rinse with hot water. Remove chicken joints and add rice to bacon and onion mix. Stir well. When cold, arrange in foil-lined casseroles with joints. Put into polythene bags and freeze. Remove dishes when food is frozen and return food to bags.

To Serve.
Remove foil and return to casserole. Reheat in moderate oven 350° Reg 4 for about 1½ hr. Garnish with watercress and serve with salad.

Storage time 3 months.   **Freezer space ¼ cu ft.**

CHICKEN AND HAM DELIGHT

To make 10 portions.

Sauce.	Ingredients.
¾ pt milk	9 oz chicken cooked
1 onion	9 oz lean ham cooked
pinch nutmeg	1 tsp made mustard
½ tsp celery salt	few drops Worcester sauce
1 oz cornflour	parsley.

Put the milk, chopped onion, celery salt and nutmeg into a pan. Bring to the boil and season to taste. Leave in a warm place to infuse for about 15 min. Then thicken with cornflour mixed to a paste with a little water and boil again, stirring all the time. Reduce heat and simmer for 2-3 min. Mince the chicken and ham finely or if blender available blend with a little of the sauce. Add meat to liquid. Stir in the parsley, mustard and Worcester sauce. When completely cold pack into individual foil containers or large containers as desired. Freeze.

To Serve.
Remove lids from containers and allow to thaw to room temperature. Serve with crisp toast as a supper snack. It also makes a delightful addition to a cold buffet. But with the addition of a green salad and brown bread it could serve as a cool meal for summer days. Perhaps if it is intended to use in this way the meat should be diced.

Storage time 3 months.   **Freezer space ¼ cu ft.**

CHICKEN A L'ORANGE

To make 8 portions.

Ingredients.

2 onions	**rind of 2 oranges and**
4 sticks celery	**juice of 4**
butter to fry	**2 tbs parsley**
8 portions chicken	**2 oz green olives.**

Chop the onions and fry in butter until just beginning to brown. Push aside and add chicken joints. Brown on all sides. Put chicken and onions into a casserole. Wash and slice the celery and add to chicken. Season to taste. Mix the orange rind and the juice with the parsley and olives. Pour this mixture over the chicken. Cover the casserole and cook for 1 hr at 350° Reg 4. When completely cold divide into individual containers or foil-lined casseroles. Put casseroles into polythene bags and freeze. Dishes can be removed when frozen. Return food to bags.

To Serve.
Remove foil and return to original casseroles or reheat in individual containers. Put casseroles into cold oven set to reach 375° Reg 5 and heat for 1½ hr. Serve with:—

Duchess Potatoes
Cream potatoes with butter and egg and season well. Pipe on to greased baking sheet and brush with milk or egg. Bake in moderately hot oven 400° Reg 6 for 25 min until golden brown.

Storage time 3 months.   **Freezer space ½ cu ft.**

CHICKEN WITH PINEAPPLE

To make 8 portions.

Ingredients.

4 oz blanched almonds
2 small onions
3 oz cornflour
2 chicken stock cubes
½ pt water

11 oz can pineapple
 rings—drained
16 oz sliced cooked
 chicken
16 oz rice, for serving.

Lightly brown almonds in oil and remove from pan. Sauté the chopped onions in the same oil. Stir in cornflour and crumble in stock cubes. Mix well. Make pineapple juice up to 1½ pt with water. Stir into pan. Bring to boil still stirring. Mix in the chicken pieces. Chop the pineapple rings and add with the almonds to the mixture. Cook for a further 3 min. Divide into foil lined dishes when completely cold and place in polythene bags to freeze. Remove dishes when food is frozen and return it to bags.

To Serve.

Remove foil and return food to original casseroles. Reheat in moderate oven 350° Reg 4. Allowing 2 oz rice per person. Boil it for 15 min in plenty of well salted water. Drain into a colander and rinse with hot water to achieve separate and fluffy grains. Garnish with pineapple pieces. If it proves necessary to open a further tin the residue can be turned into a waxed or plastic container and stored in the freezer.

Storage time 3 months.   **Freezer space ⅔ cu ft.**

CURRIED CHICKEN

To make 8 portions.

Ingredients.

4 onions	2 tbs curry powder
2 cloves garlic	8 chicken joints
cooking oil	2 (14 oz) tins tomatoes.
seasoning	

Chop the onions and crush the garlic and mix together with enough cooking oil to coat. Season well. Add curry powder stirring well. Put chicken joints into a bowl and spoon over the curry mixture. Toss well to mix. Cover and leave to stand for at least three hours. Turn into a large saucepan and add tinned tomatoes, breaking the whole fruit. Cook over a low heat, turning occasionally, until golden brown. Allow to cool. Divide into family sized, foil-lined casseroles or into individual containers. Put casseroles into polythene bags to freeze. Remove dishes when food is frozen and return to bags.

To Serve.

Turn chicken joints and sauce into a pan. Cover and simmer gently until chicken is tender, approximately 1 hr. Or return to casseroles after removing foil and heat in moderate oven 350° Reg 4 for 1½ hr. Serve with rice that has been boiled for 15 min in plenty of well salted water. Drain rice into colander and rinse with hot water to ensure separate and fluffy grains.

Storage time 3 months.   **Freezer space $\frac{2}{3}$ cu ft.**

TURKEY TROT

To make 4 portions.

Ingredients.

8 oz cooked turkey or chicken	2 oz breadcrumbs
	2 eggs
1 onion	¾ pt top of milk
4 oz cheese	seasoning.

Mince the meat and onion twice and mix with the bread-crumbs. Grate the cheese and stir into the mixture. Season. Separate the eggs. Beat the yolks with the milk and stir into the meat mixture. Beat the egg whites until stiff and fold into the mixture. Turn into a greased cas-serole and bake in a moderate oven 350° Reg 4 for 45 mins. The mixture should be risen and brown. Cool as quickly as possible and put casserole into a polythene bag to freeze. If the dish will be required, first line it with foil and then it may be removed and the frozen food returned to the bag.

To Serve.
Put into the refrigerator to thaw overnight. Garnish with slices of tomato and bake in oven at 375° Reg 5 for 30 min. Serve with green salad or crisp brown toast. An ideal recipe for those left over turkey pieces at Christmas time but chicken makes a good substitute.

Storage time 2 months.   **Freezer space ⅛ cu ft.**

HUNGARIAN GOULASH

To make 8 portions.

Ingredients.

4 onions	1 tbs paprika
2 cloves of garlic	pinch mixed herbs
2 lb braising steak	oil to fry
2 oz flour	seasoning
2 pt beef stock	lemon juice for serving.
2 tbs tomato purée	

Chop onions and garlic and fry until golden. Cut up meat and add to onions. Seal in hot oil. Add flour and stir in stock all at once. Add tomato purée and herbs and paprika. Season and bring to the boil. Put into a large casserole and cook in moderate oven 350° Reg 4 for 2-2½ hr. When completely cold divide over suitable containers and freeze.

To Serve.
Turn into a casserole and reheat in moderate oven 350° Reg 4. Diced carrots and frozen peas should be added when fully thawed. Add lemon juice just before serving. Serve with creamed potatoes.

Dumplings can be added with the vegetables. Mix 4 oz flour with 1½ oz shredded suet and a little salt. Mix to a firm dough with water and form into small balls. Drop into gravy and cook for 20 min until dumplings are risen and fluffy. Extra dumplings could be frozen till needed.

Storage time 3 months.   **Freezer space ⅛ cu ft.**

SAVOURY MINCED BEEF

To make 5 lb.

Ingredients.

1 lb onions
5 lb fresh minced beef
½ oz sugar
1 heaped tsp salt

clove of garlic (optional)
beef stock
2 tbs tomato purée.

Minced beef can often be bought in bulk quite cheaply or comes included in a bulk purchase of beef. On its own it isn't very appetising but this recipe improves it and gives one a basic mix to use in several other dishes. Chop onions and fry in oil. Add mince and stir until browned. Crush garlic and add, with salt, sugar and tomato purée. Add ½ pt beef stock and simmer for 15 min. When completely cold divide into suitable amounts and put into waxed or foil containers. Some could go direct into pastry cases and be stored as meat pies. Freeze.

To Serve.

Fill Vol au Vent cases with the mince. Bake in hot oven 450° Reg. 8.

Use savoury mince for Cottage Pie, Meat Balls, Spaghetti Bolognese or any other recipe which calls for minced beef. Children love it with the addition of a little stock and thickening, served with chips.

Storage time 3 months.   **Freezer space ¼ cu ft.**

SPAGHETTI BOLOGNESE

To make 4 portions.

Ingredients.

1 onion chopped fine	seasoning
1 clove garlic crushed	oil to fry
(optional)	1 tsp sugar
1 lb minced beef	1 tbs tomato purée
½ pt stock	1 bay leaf.

Fry onion and garlic until soft but not brown. Add tomato purée and sugar. Stir in the meat and brown before adding stock and herbs and seasoning. Allow to simmer for 20 min. Remove bay leaf and spoon sauce into foil container. Allow to cool completely before freezing.

To Serve.

Allow meat sauce to thaw then reheat gently. Cook spaghetti:—To a large panful of boiling water, add salt and spaghetti. Boil gently, stirring occasionally, for about 15 min (or until tender). Drain into a colander and pour over a small quantity of cold water to remove stickiness. Serve on a large hot plate with the meat sauce poured over it and a side dish of grated cheese, preferably Parmesan. As this amount is sufficient for only four people, treble quantities may be prepared and frozen in amounts suitable. In place of the minced beef the Savoury Mince, as prepared in a previous recipe, could be used. Reduce cooking time to 10 min as this meat has already been cooked.

Storage time 4 months.   **Freezer space ¼ cu ft.**

STEAK AND KIDNEY PUDDINGS

To make 3 family size or 12 individual portions.

Ingredients.   Filling.
Suet Crust.   2¼ lb stewing steak
1½ lb flour   12 oz kidney
1 tsp salt   seasoned stock 3 pt
12 oz shredded suet   2 tbs flour
water to mix.   oil for frying.

Cut up meat (mince for individuals), and brown in oil. Sprinkle in flour and add stock. Bring to the boil and pour into a pan. Simmer for 1½ hr.

Suet Crust. Mix suet, flour, salt and water to rolling consistency. Roll out thinly and line basins, leaving enough crust for lids. Family puddings can be made in foil lined basins, but smaller sizes may be made in foil basins. When completely cold divide meat mixture between containers and put on suet crust lids. Foil covers are supplied with small foil basins but large dishes must be placed inside polythene bags before freezing. Fasten mouth with wire twister. When frozen, remove basins and replace puddings in polythene bags. Secure.

To Serve.
Individual puddings can be boiled in foil basins but remove foil sheet from the others, while frozen, and return to basins. Cover with greaseproof paper and tie. Boil in sufficient water to reach halfway up the basins for 1½ hr.

Storage time 4 months.　　　　　**Freezer space ½ cu ft.**

STUFFED BEEF ROLLS

To make 8 portions.

Ingredients.	*Stuffing.*
Oil for frying	8 oz sausage meat
8 thin slices lean beef steak	1 onion
2 onions	1 oz margarine
2 carrots	1 oz breadcrumbs
½ pt beef stock	1 tsp sage
small tin tomatoes	1 egg.
1 clove garlic	
1 bay leaf	

Mix the sausage meat, breadcrumbs, minced onion and sage together. A little lemon rind can be added if liked. Stir in the egg. Season with salt and black pepper. Spread the stuffing over each piece of steak and roll them up, tying with fine thread. Brown the beef rolls in hot oil and put aside. Add the chopped onions and carrots and brown also. Pour in the stock, tomatoes, crushed garlic and bay leaf. Bring to the boil. Pour sauce over rolls in a casserole and cook for 1 hr at 350° Reg 4. When completely cold, put into a foil-lined casserole or waxed container and freeze. Casserole can be removed and food returned to polythene bag if desired.

To Serve.
Remove foil if necessary and return to casserole. Reheat in oven for 1½ hr. Serve with creamed potatoes and a green vegetable.

Storage time 3 months.   **Freezer space ⅛ cu ft.**

SPICY MEAT BALLS

To make 6 portions.

Ingredients.

1 lb minced beef	½ tsp black pepper
½ lb minced pork	1 onion
2 oz breadcrumbs	1 large tin tomatoes
1 egg	1 clove garlic
½ tsp sage	½ tsp coriander
½ tsp mint	cooking oil.

Mix together meat, onion and breadcrumbs. Stir in the egg, salt, all herbs except coriander and black pepper. Mix well, adding a little water if necessary to bind the mixture. Mould into balls on a floured board. Fry balls in oil until golden brown. Remove balls and leave to cool. Add crushed garlic, tomatoes and coriander and simmer for 10 min. Allow sauce to cool and pour into waxed container. Freeze. Meat balls can be frozen separately in polythene bags if extra quantities are prepared. The sauce also should be frozen in suitable sized containers.

To Serve.

Combine sufficient quantities of sauce and meat balls in a pan and heat over a gentle heat. When thawed, simmer for approximately 30 min to cook meat completely. Serve with boiled rice. Allow 2 oz per person and boil in plenty of salted water for 15-20 min. Drain into a colander and rinse with hot water to separate grains.

Storage time 3 months.　　　　**Freezer space ¼ cu ft.**

BOEUF STROGANOFF

To make 6 portions.

Ingredients.

1½ lb rump steak	6 fluid oz Beaujolais
1 oz flour	8 oz mushrooms
1 large onion	½ pt soured cream for
3 tbs oil	serving.

Cut meat into strips and coat in flour. Fry in oil until brown, approximately 10 min. Remove. Chop onion and fry for 5 min. Return meat to the pan and slowly stir in the wine. Bring to the boil and simmer for 5 min. Slice mushrooms and cook in a little butter for 5 min. Add the mushrooms to the meat and mix well. Allow to cool. An inexpensive version which is quite good, can be made with braising steak but the cooking time would have to be increased. When completely cold pack into waxed or foil containers and freeze.

To Serve.

Reheat gently over a low heat, stirring frequently. Just before serving stir in the soured cream, adjusting quantity according to amount of stroganoff being reheated. Do not allow to boil once the cream has been added. Serve with rice boiled in plenty of salted water and rinsed with hot water. Allow 2 oz of rice per person.

Storage time 3 months.　　　　**Freezer space ⅛ cu ft.**

MEAT LOAF

To make 3 loaves.

Ingredients.

3 potatoes	Pinch mixed herbs
3 carrots	3 eggs
1 large onion	3 lb minced beef.
6 oz breadcrumbs	

Grate vegetables or put through a fine mincer. Mix with breadcrumbs, meat, herbs and eggs. Season to taste. Press mixture into foil lined loaf tins. Cover with greaseproof paper. Bake in oven at 400° Reg 6 for 45 min. Cool in tins and when completely cold put tins into polythene bags and freeze. Tins may be removed when frozen. Return food to bags.

To Serve.

Allow loaves to thaw to room temperature approximately 6 hr. Before completely thawed, cut slices from loaf for neater results. Serve with salad or as a sandwich filling. If thicker slices are cut they can be warmed through in a slow oven 300° Reg 2 and served with gravy and vegetables. Savoury Mince could be substituted for the minced beef in this recipe, omitting the onions. Such a loaf would not need such a long cooking time. Children love slices of meat loaf fried in hot fat and served with chips. Or put between bread rolls and toasted.

Storage time 1 month.   **Freezer space $\frac{1}{4}$ cu ft.**

SWEET AND SOUR MEAT BALLS

To make 12 portions.

Ingredients.

1½ lb minced beef
6 oz breadcrumbs
3 eggs
3 small onions
3 carrots
3 leeks
6 sticks celery
6 oz mushrooms

3 tsp cornflour
6 tsp sugar
¾ pt water
3 dsp tomato ketchup
3 tbs vinegar
6 tsp soy sauce
seasoning.

Mix meat, breadcrumbs and eggs together. Season and shape into 48 balls on a floured board. Fry the meat balls in hot oil browning all over. Lift out to drain on kitchen paper. Chop onions and cut carrots into strips. Slice leeks and celery and mushrooms. Fry vegetables slowly. Mix the cornflour, sugar and water, and add ketchup, vinegar and soy sauce. Pour into pan with vegetables. Cook for 15 min stirring occasionally. Allow to cool. Pack sauce into waxed containers in suitable amounts. Freeze. Put balls on to trays, not touching, and place trays in polythene bags. Freeze, then repack in bags.

To Serve.
Empty sauce into a pan and heat over low light. When thawed, add meat balls and cover and simmer for 20 min. Serve with rice boiled in plenty of salted water. 2 oz per person.

Storage time 3 months.   **Freezer space ¼ cu ft.**

RICH BEEF CASSEROLE

To make 12 portions.

Ingredients.

3 lb chuck steak

3 tbs flour (seasoned)

3 onions

dried mixed herbs

2 cups beef stock

1 cup red wine

oil to fry.

Cut meat into large chunks and coat in seasoned flour. Brown in hot oil. Put meat into large casserole. Slice onions and fry in the same oil, until soft but not brown and add to meat. Sprinkle over the herbs and add stock and wine. Cover casserole and cook for 2½ hr at 350° Reg 4. When completely cold, divide into suitably sized waxed or foil containers or foil-lined dishes. Remove dishes when food is frozen and return food to polythene bags.

To Serve.

Remove foil, if used, and return to casserole to heat in oven at 350° Reg 4 for 1 hr. Or reheat in a saucepan, stirring frequently. Serve with dumplings. Mix 4 oz flour with 1½ oz of shredded suet and mix to a firm dough with water. Add a little salt. Mould into balls and add to simmering stew. Cook for 15-20 min.

Storage time 3 months.   **Freezer space ⅜ cu ft.**

BEEF AND TOMATO CASSEROLE

To make 8 portions.

Ingredients.

oil for frying
4 onions
2 lb stewing steak
¼ pt beef stock

two 14 oz tins tomatoes
2 tbs tomato purée
cornflour
½ tsp marjoram.

Slice onions and cut meat into cubes. Fry meat and onions in oil. Add stock, tomatoes and purée and marjoram. Half a teaspoon of sugar brings out the flavour of the purée. Season and bring to the boil. Thicken with cornflour. Return to boil stirring. Transfer to casserole to complete cooking in moderate oven 350° Reg 4 for 2 hrs. Allow to cool completely and spoon into waxed or foil containers of practical sizes. Freeze.

To Serve.

Turn into a saucepan and reheat over a low heat. Or return to a casserole and heat in a moderate oven 350° Reg 4 for 1 hr. Serve with boiled potatoes and carrots. Packs of stewing steak can be bought at reduced prices per 5 lb pack. This makes an ideal chain recipe to use such steak. Thus saving on both initial cost and fuel costs, while producing a tasty meal from the cheaper cuts. Dumplings may be added if desired.

Storage time 3 months.   **Freezer space ¼ cu ft.**

BEEF AND PASTA CASSEROLE

To make 4 portions.

Ingredients.

oil for frying	seasoning
1 lb minced beef or	3 tomatoes
Savoury Mince	¼ pt stock
2 onions	cornflour
1 clove garlic	1 tbs parsley
½ lb macaroni	2 tbs tomato purée.
½ pt white cheese sauce	

If Savoury Mince is used omit the onions and allow mince to thaw. Use as fresh mince but reduce cooking time. Chop onions and crush garlic and fry without browning. Add meat and brown. Stir in the chopped tomatoes and purée. Add the stock and parsley. Season to taste. Cover and simmer for 10 mins. Thicken with cornflour. Meanwhile cook the macaroni in well salted water for 15 min. Drain and arrange in alternate layers with the meat mixture in a casserole. Last layer to be macaroni. Make a cheese sauce with ½ pt milk thickened with cornflour and 2 oz grated cheese. Pour sauce over macaroni. When completely cold place dish in a polythene bag and freeze. If foil has been used to line the casserole it can be removed when food is frozen. Return food to bag.

To Serve.
Remove foil and return food to original dish. Bake in oven set to reach 400° Reg 6 for 45 min timed from reaching correct temperature. Cheese topping should be slightly brown.

Storage time 3 months.   **Freezer space ⅛ cu ft.**

CURRY BURGERS

To make 15 portions.

Ingredients.

2 small onions	4 tsp curry powder
2 lb minced beef	6 tbs milk
4 oz white breadcrumbs	2 eggs.

Mince the meat finely and mix with the breadcrumbs and minced onions. Stir in the curry powder mixing well. Beat the eggs into milk and stir into the mixture. Form into approximately fifteen burgers on a floured board. Coat with flour and place between layers of foil or grease-proof paper so that the burgers don't touch. Freeze. When frozen pack into polythene bags.

To Serve.
Fry one burger per person in hot oil, turning to brown on both sides. Place slices of tomato and onion rings on top and put under a hot grill after brushing with melted margarine. Served with chipped potatoes. If preferred, a slice of processed cheese could be substituted for the tomato and the whole served with a green salad. This is an ideal recipe for chain-cooking when a large amount of minced beef has been bought. The burgers take little space but provide a quick and easily served snack.

Storage time 3 months. **Freezer space $\frac{1}{8}$ cu ft.**

BROWN BEEF STEW

To make 12 portions.

Ingredients.

oil for frying	cornflour
2 lb onions	3 lb shin beef
2 lb carrots	bouquet garni.
2 pt beef stock	

Chop onions and fry in a little oil until brown. Remove onions and cut shin beef into cubes. Fry in the hot oil to brown. Add the beef stock, stirring. Cut the carrots into slices and add along with the onions and the bouquet garni. Bring to the boil. Season to taste and thicken with cornflour. Cover and simmer for 2 hr. Remove the bouquet garni. Allow to cool and skim off any excess fat. Pack into waxed or foil cartons in practical amounts. Freeze.

To Serve.

Return to saucepan and reheat slowly. Dumplings may be added. Mix 4 oz flour with 1½ oz shredded suet and salt to a firm dough with water. Roll into balls and drop into simmering stew. Cook for 15-20 min. Serve with boiled potatoes. Buying meat in bulk for a freezer often means taking a quantity of the cheaper cuts which seem a little uninteresting. This recipe could be made up when the beef arrives and put down as a useful standby. It could also serve as a basis for other dishes.

Storage time 3 months.   **Freezer space ½ cu ft.**

MILD BEEF CURRY

To make 8 portions.

Ingredients.

2 lb stewing steak	1 oz cornflour
2 large onions	2 oz sultanas
1½ tbs curry powder	1 pt beef stock
1 tbs tomato ketchup	seasoning
1 tbs golden syrup	oil to fry
1 tbs sweet chutney	2 large cooking apples.

Chop onions and fry with meat cut into pieces, until meat is browned. Blend curry powder, ketchup, syrup and chutney together. Stir in cornflour. Add the curry mixture to the meat, stirring well. Chop the apples and add, along with the sultanas. Stir in the stock. Bring to the boil and season to taste. Simmer gently for 2 hr in a covered pan. When completely cold pour into suitable wax or foil containers and freeze. The curry sauce can be prepared without the meat to be used later to enhance any left-over meats. In this event cook sauce for 30 mins. only.

To Serve.
Return the curry to a saucepan and reheat slowly. Serve with plain boiled rice. Allowing 2 oz per person, boil in plenty of salted water for 15 min. Drain and rinse with hot water to separate grains. If the sauce is meatless, reheat and add meat once the sauce is thawed. Allow time to heat meat all through. Serve with rice.

Storage time 3 months.   **Freezer space ¼ cu ft.**

CHILI-CON-CARNE

To make 8 portions.

Ingredients.

oil for frying	4 tbs tomato purée
2 onions	1 tsp chili powder
2 cloves garlic	pinch marjoram
2 lb minced beef	two 8 oz tins baked beans
two 8 oz tins tomatoes	for serving.

Chop onions, crush garlic, and put with the minced beef into a saucepan in which a little oil has been heated. Fry until meat browns. Stir in tomatoes, breaking any whole fruit with a fork and add tomato purée, chili powder and marjoram. Bring to the boil and season to taste. Cover and simmer for 30 min. If some is to be eaten, separate the amount, empty can of beans into pan and allow to simmer for a further 5 min. Put surplus to cool. When surplus is completely cold, pack into waxed or foil containers and freeze.

To Serve.
Turn into a saucepan and add baked beans. Reheat over a low heat stirring occasionally. Serve with creamed potatoes. Or allow 2 oz rice per person and boil in plenty of salted water for 15 min. Drain into a colander and rinse with hot water to separate grains.

Storage time 3 months.   **Freezer space ¼ cu ft.**

QUICK CURRIED STEAK

To make 8 portions.

Ingredients.

oil for frying	1 tsp ground ginger
2 lbs stewing steak	1 tsp cinnamon
2 onions	2 tsp curry powder
4 oz mushrooms	1 clove garlic
6 tomatoes	celery salt
½ pt stock or water	mixed herbs.
1 pepper	

Cut steak into cubes and dip in seasoned flour. Fry in hot oil for 5 min until brown. Remove, and place in a casserole. Fry onions, tomatoes, pepper and mushrooms in remaining oil. Add garlic and fry for 1 minute. Add cinnamon, ginger and curry. Stir in ½ pt stock or water and bring to the boil. Transfer to casserole and cook in a moderate oven, 350° Reg 4 for 2 hr. When completely cold put into foil-lined casserole or waxed container and freeze.

To Serve.

Remove foil if necessary, and return to casserole. Warm in moderate oven 350° Reg 4 for 1 hr, or heat over low heat in a saucepan, stirring frequently. Serve with boiled rice. Allow 2 oz rice per person and boil in plenty of salted water for 15 min. Drain and rinse with hot water to separate grains. Garnish with one or more of the following:—Grated cheese, Dessicated coconut. Raw onion rings. Green salad. Yogurt. Sliced pineapple. Mango chutney.

Storage time 3 months.   **Freezer space ¼ cu ft.**

ROSEMARY LAMB SLICES

To make 8 portions.

Ingredients.

2 tsp rosemary	seasoning
3 oz breadcrumbs	oil to fry
1 egg	1 onion for serving.
8 thick slices cold lamb	

Mix rosemary with breadcrumbs and seasoning, stirring well. Break egg into shallow dish and beat. Dip lamb slices in egg and coat with breadcrumbs. Fry lamb slices in hot oil for one minute on each side. Drain on kitchen paper and when completely cold wrap in foil and freeze. For those slices that are to be eaten directly, fry onion rings until golden to garnish dish.

To Serve.
Place lamb slices in hot oil and reheat taking care not to overbrown. Crisply fry onion rings and serve with lamb slices and accompany with redcurrant jelly.* Serve with a green salad and any of the commercially packed crisps or maize sticks. Alternatively, boil rice in plenty of water flavoured with chicken stock cubes, and strips of green or red pepper added. Allow 2 oz per person. Drain and rinse with hot water to separate grains.

Storage time 3 months.　　　　**Freezer space minimal.**

* See "The Right Way to Make Jams," uniform with this book.

LAMB PIE

To make 6 portions.

Ingredients.

1 lb boned lamb	6 ripe tomatoes
1 small onion	8 oz puff pastry (frozen)
5 oz frozen peas	4 lambs' kidneys.

Cut lamb into small pieces and slice and core kidneys. Coat in flour. Finely chop onion. Pour boiling water over tomatoes to loosen skins. Fry onion for 2 min. Add lamb and kidney and brown. Add tomatoes, peas and 3 tbs water. Bring to the boil and season to taste. Allow to cool. Roll out the puff pastry. Put cold lamb mixture into foil-lined pie dish and place pastry lid on top. Put dish into polythene bag and freeze. Dish may be removed when frozen. Return food to polythene bag.

To Serve.

Remove foil and return pie to original dish. Put into a cold oven set at 400° Reg 6. Allow correct temperature to be reached and then cook for 30 min until crust is golden brown and risen. As with all pies it is more economical to freeze uncooked. The pastry does not suffer from being put into a cold oven contrary to old beliefs. The filling thaws as oven reaches temperature.

Storage time 3 months.   **Freezer space $\frac{1}{8}$ cu ft.**

LAMB CASSEROLE

To make 6 portions.

Ingredients.

2 breasts of lamb boned
2 lb potatoes
½ lb carrots
1 small onion
½ pt beef stock

Stuffing.
½ lb sausage meat
1 egg
1 tsp mint
4 oz breadcrumbs
seasoning.

Put sausage meat, egg, mint and breadcrumbs into a bowl and mix well. Season well. Spread stuffing over lamb breasts and roll up. Tie with string in four places and cut between strings to make eight rolls. Peel and slice potatoes. Cook carrots in a little water and chop. Chop onion. Arrange vegetables in layers in a large casserole and place rolls on top. Pour over the stock. Cover and cook in moderate oven 350° Reg 4 for 30 min. When completely cold put into foil or waxed cartons and freeze.

To Serve.
Return to casserole and reheat in moderate oven 350° Reg 4 from cold for approximately 1 hr. When heated through remove string from rolls and serve with extra potatoes if required.

It is a good plan to make up this recipe when lamb is delivered. If the breast is frozen it often gets forgotten.

Storage time 3 months.   **Freezer space ⅛ cu ft.**

LAMB CURRY

To make 4 portions.

Ingredients.

8 neck chops	1 tbs mango chutney
1 large onion	2 tbs curry powder
1 cooking apple	oil to fry
1 tbs cornflour	1 tbs lemon juice
1 pt chicken stock	1 tbs jam.

Bone meat and cut into pieces. Fry in hot oil for 5 min till brown. Remove and add chopped onions and curry powder. Fry for 5 min. Stir in the cornflour and add the stock. Stir in the chopped apple, the jam and lemon juice and the chutney. Bring to the boil, still stirring. Cover and simmer for 1¼ hr. Allow to cool completely and pack into waxed or foil containers. Freeze.

To Serve.
Boil 2 oz rice per person in plenty of salted water for approximately 15 min while curry is reheating in a saucepan over a low heat. Drain rice into a colander and rinse with hot water to separate grains. Arrange rice round a serving dish and pour curry into centre.
Serve curry with one or more of the following:—Grated cheese. Dessicated coconut. Raw onion rings. Green salad. Yogurt. Sliced pineapple. Mango chutney.
Curry that has been frozen may lose a little of the curry flavour, so taste and add more curry powder on thawing.

Storage time 2 months. **Freezer space ⅛ cu ft.**

SAVOURY LAMB STEW

To make 4 portions.

Ingredients.

8 pieces middle neck	$\frac{3}{4}$ pt water
1 large carrot	2 tsp tomato purée
1 medium parsnip	8 oz tin butter beans
1 leek	seasoning.
oil to fry	

Dip the neck chops in a little seasoned flour and fry to brown for 2-3 min. Add water and liquid from butter beans to pan and thicken with cornflour. Season to taste. Stir in the tomato purée and bring to the boil. Dice the carrots and slice leek and parsnip and add vegetables to meat. Simmer for 1 hr. Add butter beans and cook for 5 min. When completely cold put into waxed or foil containers and freeze.

To Serve.

Turn into saucepan and heat over gentle heat or put into a casserole and reheat in moderate oven 350° Reg 4. Test to see chops are thoroughly cooked. Serve with boiled potatoes.

This is an ideal recipe for using the cheaper chops on buying a full lamb for home freezing. Many people argue that it is uneconomical to buy the full lamb because one has to take the cheap cuts. But this, and other recipes included, disprove that theory.

Storage time 3 months.   **Freezer space $\frac{1}{8}$ cu ft.**

MOUSSAKA

To make 4 portions.

Ingredients.	Sauce.
12 oz cooked lamb	1 oz margarine
2 tsp tomato purée	1 oz flour
½ pt stock	½ pt milk
4 aubergines	black pepper
6 oz grated hard cheese	1 egg
oil to fry	1 onion.

Chop the onion and fry in a little oil until soft. Add the lamb, minced, and seasoning, tomato purée and stock. Bring to the boil and simmer for 5-10 min. Peel and slice the aubergines and fry in oil adding more oil as they soak it up. Put aubergines in bottom of casserole and sprinkle with some of the cheese. Add a second layer of aubergines, reserving some. Spoon the meat mixture on top, and add rest of aubergines. Make the sauce by melting the margarine and stirring in the flour. Cook for a minute and gradually add milk, beating well. Bring to the boil and season to taste. Remove from the heat and beat in the egg. Pour the sauce over the Moussaka. Sprinkle over rest of cheese. Allow to cool and freeze.

To Serve.
Remove foil if used, and return to casserole. Cook in a moderate oven 350° Reg 4 for 30-35 min until bubbling and brown. Serve with green salad.

Storage time 3 months. **Freezer space ⅛ cu ft.**

LAMB ITALIENNE

To make 4 portions.

Ingredients.

oil for frying
1 medium onion
2 carrots
2 sticks celery
8 best neck chops
1 tbs cornflour
15 oz tin tomatoes
seasoning

$\frac{1}{4}$ pt water
1 tsp mixed herbs
black pepper

Parsley Dumplings.
4 oz flour
1$\frac{1}{2}$ oz shredded suet
1 tbs parsley.

Slice the onion and fry in oil. Dice carrots and chop celery. Add to the onion and fry for 2-3 min. Remove and place in shallow casserole. Brown chops in remaining oil and arrange on top of veg. Mix tomatoes with water and herbs in saucepan and bring to the boil. Season to taste, thicken with cornflour, and pour over lamb and vegetables. Cook in moderate oven 350° Reg. 4 for $\frac{1}{2}$ hr. Meanwhile make dumplings. Mix suet, salt, flour and parsley to a firm dough with water. Form into eight balls. Put to freeze on trays without touching and put trays in polythene bags. When completely cold put casserole in bag and freeze. Remove dish and trays when frozen. Return food to bags.

To Serve.
Remove foil and return to casserole. Heat in moderate oven, 350° Reg 4. When thawed, add dumplings and cook a further 15-20 min. Serve with boiled potatoes or spaghetti.

Storage time 3 months.　　　　　**Freezer space $\frac{1}{8}$ cu ft.**

LAMB WITH A TANG

To make 5 portions.

Ingredients.

1 lb cooked lamb	2 large onions
1 clove garlic	10 oz rice
juice of 1 lemon	1 inch stick cinnamon
1 tbs curry powder	1 tsp black pepper
6 oz margarine	1 hard boiled egg for serving
¼ pt yoghurt	1 tomato for serving.

Cut lamb into cubes and put into a bowl with lemon juice, seasoning and yoghurt. Add curry powder and crushed garlic. Leave to marinate for 30 min. Fry chopped onions in hot margarine for 5 min until crisp. Crush, and add to lamb mixture. Cook rice with cinnamon and black pepper in plenty of water. Drain and rinse with hot water and put aside to cool. Put meat into foil lined casserole and cover with cold rice. Melt rest of margarine and pour over the rice. Allow to cool and place in a polythene bag and freeze. Remove dish when frozen and return food to bag.

To Serve.
Remove foil and return to original casserole. Place in cold oven set to 300° Reg 2. Cook for 1½-2 hr, timed from when correct temperature is reached. Garnish with slices of hard boiled egg and tomatoes. Crisp fry onion rings for further garnish. Service with a green salad.

Storage time 3 months. **Freezer space ⅛ cu ft.**

VEGETABLE AND LAMB CASSEROLE

To make 8 portions.

Ingredients.

oil for frying	1 onion
3 lb stewing lamb	½ pt stock
4 oz butter beans	4 sticks celery
large tin tomatoes	¼ tsp chili powder.
3 carrots	

Beans should have soaked overnight. Brown the meat in a little oil and stir in the chili powder. Add ½ pt stock and the tinned tomatoes and drained beans. Season to taste and cover. Simmer for 1 hr. Dice the carrots, chop the onion and celery and stir into the meat. Simmer for a further 30 min. Thicken with cornflour if necessary. When completely cold put into a waxed or foil container and freeze.

To Serve.

Return to pan and reheat over a gentle heat until thoroughly heated. Serve with boiled potatoes. The chili powder gives this dish its own special taste but if not liked, black pepper will add a spicy taste. When cheap, fresh tomatoes may be used, but a little more stock may be necessary. If practical, leave the addition of vegetables until the reheating process. In this way they are not cooked twice.

Storage time 3 months.   **Freezer space ⅛ cu ft.**

LAMB SURPRISE

To make 4 portions.

Ingredients.
oil for frying
4 chump or loin chops
1 small onion
4 rashers streaky bacon
2 oz mushrooms.

Pastry.
8 oz flour
4 oz lard and margarine
salt.

Chop onion and cut bacon into strips. Chop mushrooms. Fry bacon for a little but do not crisp. Add mushrooms and fry for 2 min. Allow to cool. Make pastry by rubbing fat into flour and salt and mixing with water to a firm dough. Cut into four pieces and roll out each piece into a six inch round. Divide the cold stuffing mixture between each pastry round and lay chop on top. Dampen edges of pastry and fold round chop sealing edges. Wrap each parcel in foil and freeze in polythene bags.

To Serve.
Remove foil and place lamb parcel on a greased baking sheet. Brush with beaten egg. Put into a cold oven set at 350° Reg 4 and bake for 1½ hr from when temperature is reached. Raise heat for final 10 min to brown crust. Scrub potatoes and place round the parcels to bake in their jackets. When cooked, cut a slit in each and put in a knob of butter; or serve with creamed potatoes and a thick mushroom sauce (made by heating a tin of condensed mushroom soup and adding a little water to thin).

Storage time 3 months.   **Freezer space ⅛ cu ft.**

LAMBURGERS

To make 12 burgers.

Ingredients.

2 onions	2 oz fresh breadcrumbs
1 tsp rosemary	2 dsp parsley
2 eggs	seasoning.
2 lb minced cooked lamb	

Chop onion. Beat eggs in a bowl and add the onion, rosemary, lamb and breadcrumbs. Sprinkle in the parsley. Mix well and season to taste. Shape into twelve rounds on a floured board and coat with flour. Place on flat trays without touching and put trays into polythene bags. Freeze. When frozen store in polythene bags.

To Serve.

Fry lamburgers in hot oil for ten to fifteen minutes turning once to brown both sides. Warm a bread roll for each lamburger and split in half. Place lamburger in slit along with fried onion slices, if liked, or redcurrant jelly. Wrap in a paper napkin and serve. Alternatively, serve with green salad, or chips and baked beans. Buying in bulk often means cooking bigger joints and this recipe is an ideal way of serving left-over lamb. Sliced lamb freezes well if covered with gravy or sauce.

Storage time 1 month. **Freezer space ⅛ cu ft.**

LAMB AND TOMATO STEW

To make 8 portions.

Ingredients.

oil for frying	1 tin tomatoes
1½ lb scrag end of lamb	1 pt stock
2 onions	½-1 lb carrots
1 oz barley	pinch mixed herbs.

Bone the meat and cut into cubes. Fry in oil. Slice onions and fry with meat but do not brown. Drain liquid from the barley which has been soaking overnight and add barley to the pan. Stir in the tinned tomatoes. Pour in the stock. Add sliced carrots. Bring to the boil and season to taste adding pinch of herbs. Simmer for 1½ hr. Allow to cool and skim off excess fat. Pack into waxed or foil containers and freeze.

To Serve.

Turn stew into saucepan and reheat over a low heat. Serve with boiled potatoes. Dumplings may be added if liked. Mix 4 oz flour with 1½ oz shredded suet and pinch of salt into a firm dough with water. Form into balls and drop into simmering stew. Cook for 15-20 min. If extra quantities of dumplings are made they can be frozen uncooked on trays and stored in polythene bags.

Storage time 3 months.   **Freezer space ⅛ cu ft.**

STUFFED BREAST OF LAMB

To make 6 portions.

Ingredients.

2 breasts	1 tbs chopped mint
½ lb pork sausage meat	seasoning.
2 oz raisins	

Bone the meat. Mix raisins, sausage meat and mint together. Season to taste. Spread this stuffing over meat. Roll and tie with string firmly. Lay rolls in roasting tin. Sufficient fat will come from breast to cook it. Cover with foil. Bake for 20 min at 425° Reg 7. With meat to be eaten directly, put tomatoes round rolls for last 10 min. Remove from roaster and drain off surplus fat. When completely cold wrap in foil and put into a polythene bag to freeze.

To Serve.

Can be eaten cold with salad. Allow to thaw to room temperature and slice. Or cut thicker slices and reheat in a little stock which can then be thickened to make a gravy. Or place the frozen rolls in a roaster and add a little oil or fat. Roast to reheat and put whole tomatoes round for last five or ten minutes. Serve as a roast joint with potatoes and green vegetables. An ideal recipe for using the breast that comes with the purchase of a full lamb.

Storage time 2 months.   **Freezer space ⅛ cu ft.**

LAMB CHOPS A LA PROVENCALE

To make 4 portions.

Ingredients.

oil for frying
8 neck chops
1 tin tomatoes

clove of garlic
1 onion
seasoning.

Brown chops in hot oil and remove. Fry onion cut into rings in fat and crush garlic clove and add to pan. Stir in the tinned tomatoes breaking up the whole fruit. Season to taste. Pour mixture over chops in foil lined casserole and allow to cool completely. Place casserole in a polythene bag and freeze. Remove casserole when frozen. Return food to bag.

To Serve.

Remove foil and return to original casserole. Put into a cold oven set at 350° Reg 4. Cook for 1½ hr to cook meat thoroughly. Sliced potatoes can be placed on top of meat or baked potatoes arranged round dish. Scrub potatoes and dry before placing in oven. When cooked, split skin, and place a knob of butter in each potato. This whole meal can be put into a preset oven to be ready on your return. The chops can also be served with rice. Allow 2 oz per person and boil in plenty of salted water. Rinse with hot water to separate grains.

Storage time 3 months.   Freezer space ⅛ cu ft.

LOIN OF LAMB WITH ORANGE

To make 4 portions.

Ingredients.

8 round neck chops	**1 tbs parsley**
1 orange	**2 oz butter.**
watercress, for serving	

Grate rind from half the orange and peel this and other half and cut into slices, cutting each slice into four pieces. Heat grill to moderate. Mix orange rind and some of the flesh in a basin with butter. Season and spread over one side of chops. Grill for 7-8 min. Turn over and spread rest of orange butter on this side. Grill again. Place in a foil lined casserole and pour over juices from grill pan. Allow to cool and put casserole into a polythene bag and freeze. Remove casserole when frozen and return food to bag.

To Serve.

Remove foil and return to casserole. Reheat in moderate oven 350° Reg 4 for 30 min. Scrub small potatoes and bake alongside the casserole. Prepare garnish for chops. Take half an orange and remove alternate segments. Fill these with watercress and place in centre of serving dish. When potatoes are cooked split the skin and put in a knob of butter.

Storage time 3 months. **Freezer space ⅛ cu ft.**

PAPRIKA LAMB

To make 8 portions.

Ingredients.

3 lb lamb from shoulder
4 oz butter
½ tsp salt
1 tbs paprika
2 onions
2 tbs flour
bouquet garni
6 fl oz white wine

½ pt chicken stock
2 tbs tomato purée
8 oz mushrooms

For serving:
10 fl oz double cream
2 tbs chopped parsley.

Cut meat into cubes and brown in 3 oz of the butter. Add chopped onions and salt and paprika and mix well. Sprinkle in the flour and pour over the wine stirring well. Bring to the boil and simmer for 5 min. Add stock and tomato purée and bouquet garni. Simmer for 30 min with lid on. Gently fry the mushrooms in a little butter. Take the meat from the saucepan and put on one side. Reduce sauce to half quantity by boiling briskly. When everything is cold remove bouquet garni and put meat and sauce into a waxed container. Freeze.

To Serve.
Return food to saucepan and reheat over a low heat. When thawed, simmer for 20 min. Add the cream and bring to the boil. Sprinkle in the chopped parsley before serving. Adjust amounts of cream and parsley to amount of meat being reheated. Serve with noodles and green salad. Noodles should be boiled in salted water for 15-20 min.

Storage time 3 months.   **Freezer space ⅛ cu ft.**

IRISH STEW

To make 4 portions.

Ingredients.

1 lb middle neck of lamb or
   mutton
2 lb potatoes
3 onions

chopped parsley, for serving
seasoning
½ pt stock.

Cut meat into pieces. Slice the potatoes and onions and put alternate layers of vegetables and meat into deep casserole dish. Season well and finish with a layer of potatoes. Add stock to half depth of dish and cover. Put into oven set at 350° Reg 4 and cook for 2 hr. Or simmer gently in saucepan for 1½-2 hr. When completely cold turn into foil-lined casserole or waxed containers and freeze. If casserole is used, secure in polythene bag. Casserole may be removed on freezing.

To Serve.
Remove foil and return to original casserole or turn into saucepan. Reheat over gentle heat or put casserole into oven at 350° Reg 4. When heated through put meat joints into centre of serving dish and arrange potatoes and onions round. Sprinkle with parsley and serve. Breast of lamb, provided it is not too fat, can be prepared in the same way. Skim off excess fat on cooling before freezing.

Storage time 3 months.   **Freezer space ⅛ cu ft.**

SPICY LAMB KIDNEYS

To make 4 portions.

Ingredients.

1 large onion	1 tbs redcurrant jelly
8 skinned lambs kidneys	cornflour
4 oz button mushrooms	½ pt beef stock.
2 tbs H.P. sauce	

Chop onion and fry in a little oil. Remove cores from kidneys and cut meat in half. Add this to onions and fry. Cut mushrooms into quarters and fry, stirring mixture occasionally. Add the H.P. sauce. Pour in stock and bring to the boil. Thicken with cornflour mixed to a paste in a little water. Return to the boil and simmer for 15 min. Add redcurrant jelly and season to taste. Cook for a further 5 min. When completely cold put into waxed or foil containers and freeze.

To Serve.

Turn into a saucepan and reheat over a gentle heat until heated through. Serve with a ring of piped creamed potatoes or rice. Allowing 2 oz rice per person, boil in plenty of water and rinse with hot water to separate grains. Or heat kidneys in moderate oven 350° Reg 4 and pipe creamed potatoes on to a baking sheet. Raise temperature to 400° Reg 6 to brown potato whirls.

Storage time 1 month.   **Freezer space ⅛ cu ft.**

TRIPE AND ONIONS

To make 8 portions.

Ingredients.

2 lb tripe
2 onions
cornflour.

1 pt milk
seasoning.

Tripe in Lancashire is bought ready cooked. It is a delicacy often served cold with a salad. But further south it requires long, slow cooking. Boil in salted water for approximately 2 hr. Now treat both types the same. Chop the onions and boil in salted water until tender. Add milk and bring to the boil. Season to taste and thicken with cornflour. Make the sauce a little thicker at this stage as water will run from the tripe when added. Cut the tripe into pieces and put into sauce. Bring to the boil and allow to cool before freezing in waxed containers.

To Serve.

Turn sauce into pan and reheat slowly. Meanwhile boil sufficient potatoes and mash with milk and butter. Pour over the hot tripe and onions. Grilled sausages turn this into a meal for a gourmet. Alternatively, serve with crisp french bread for an unusual supper party dish. Chopped tomatoes may be added for colour when reheating. Or a pinch of mixed herbs for added flavour.

Storage time 3 months.   **Freezer space $\frac{1}{4}$ cu ft.**

SPANISH PORK

To make 4 portions.

Ingredients.

oil for frying	**1 green pepper**
4 pork chops	**8 oz tin tomatoes**
2 onions	**chicken stock cube**
2 tsp Worcester sauce.	**seasoned flour.**

Dip chops in seasoned flour and brown in hot oil. Remove to a casserole dish and chop onions to fry in remaining oil. Add pepper and tinned tomatoes and simmer for 10 min. Stir in the sauce and season to taste. Crumble in a chicken stock cube. Pour over the chops and cover. Cook in a moderate oven 350° Reg 4 for 1 hr. Allow to cool completely and freeze, either in a foil-lined casserole or waxed or foil container. Casserole may be removed on freezing. Return food to polythene bag.

To Serve.

Remove foil and return to casserole. Reheat in moderate oven 350° Reg 4 for about 1 hr. Serve with creamed potatoes or rice. Allow 2 oz rice per person and boil in plenty of salted water for 15 min. Drain and rinse with hot water to separate grains. Lamb chops could be treated in the same way using the best end of neck. Serve the lamb chops with spaghetti. Boil in plenty of salted water and drain. Rinse spaghetti with cold water to remove stickiness.

Storage time 3 months.   **Freezer space ⅛ cu ft.**

CASSEROLE OF PORK

To make 8 portions.

Ingredients.

8 fairly thin spare rib pork chops	seasoning
2 teacups stock or cider	6 oz sage and onion stuffing mix for serving.
6 sticks celery	

Put the pork chops into a casserole and pour over stock or cider. The cider makes a richer gravy for those who prefer it. Wash and chop the celery and add to casserole. Cover and cook in a moderate oven 350° Reg 4 for 1¾ hr. Allow to cool completely and put into family sized containers or another foil-lined casserole. Freeze. Remove dish on freezing if required.

To Serve.

Remove foil and return to original casserole or reheat in containers if heat-proof. Place in cold oven set to 400° Reg 6. While the meat is heating, make up a quantity of stuffing mix (3 oz per four persons). Bring casserole from oven and spread stuffing on top of meat. Dot with knobs of butter and return to oven. Remove lid for final 10 min to brown stuffing crust. Potatoes, scrubbed, and baked in their jackets alongside the meat make an ideal accompanying dish. When cooked, cut a cross in each potato and add a large knob of butter.

Storage time 2 months. **Freezer space ¼ cu ft.**

APPLE AND APRICOT STUFFED PORK

To make 10 portions.

Ingredients.

4 oz pkt sage and onion stuffing	1 oz fat
2½-3 lb belly pork	2 oz drd prunes
1 large cooking apple	1 oz drd apricots.

You need all but one tablespoon of stuffing mixed as directed. Leave to stand for 15 min. Peel and dice apples and add half the stuffing. Stir well. Chop the prunes and apricots and add to other half of stuffing. Line a large casserole with foil, allowing foil to stand above sides of dish. Lay 2 or 3 strips of pork in dish and cover with apple flavoured stuffing. Then put in more strips of pork and cover with apricot stuffing. Continue in layers ending with pork. Dot with knobs of fat and roast in hot oven 400° Reg 6 for 1½ hrs. Remove foil parcel from dish and when completely cold, wrap-over surplus foil and put into a polythene bag to freeze.

To Serve.

Remove foil and allow to thaw to room temperature if the meat is to be eaten cold. Either way, slice before complete thawing has taken place. Slices can be served with salad or reheated in casserole at 350° Reg 4. Prepare a thick gravy with stock cube and serve with creamed potatoes. A delicious recipe to make with the belly pork one must get on buying a full or half pig.

Storage time 2 months.   **Freezer space ⅜ cu ft.**

RABBIT CASSEROLE

To make 8 portions.

Ingredients.
oil for frying
1 large onion
rabbit cut into eight
1 pt chicken stock
2 tbs Worcester sauce
1 dsp cornflour.

Dumplings.
4 oz S.R. flour
$1\frac{1}{2}$ oz shredded suet
$\frac{1}{4}$ tsp salt
water to mix.

Chop onion and fry in oil in saucepan. Do not brown. Coat joints in flour and fry, turning to brown. Add stock and Worcester sauce and bring to the boil, stirring occasionally. Season to taste. Reduce heat and simmer for 1 hr. Make dumplings by mixing flour and suet and salt together into a soft dough with the water. Form into balls. Place dumplings on tray, not touching, to freeze. Then transfer to polythene bag. When rabbit is completely cold turn into foil-lined casserole or waxed container. Freeze.

To Serve.
Remove foil, if necessary, and return to casserole. Place in cold oven set to 350° Reg 4 for 30 min. Raise heat to 400° Reg 6 and put in the dumplings. Cook for further 20 min until dumplings are risen and fluffy. Alternatively, reheat in saucepan, adding dumplings when meal is thawed. If frozen in individual portions, any amount of dumplings can be removed and cooked as desired if they are frozen separately as directed.

Storage time 3 months.   **Freezer space $\frac{1}{4}$ cu ft.**

RABBIT COBBLER

To make 4 portions.

Ingredients.	*Cobbler.*
1 onion	6 oz self raising flour
4 rabbit joints	½ tsp salt
1 dsp cornflour	1½ oz margarine
5 oz mixed peas and carrots	¼ pt milk (scant).
oil to fry	
1 pt chicken stock.	

Fry rabbit joints in oil, browning on all sides. Remove and place in casserole. Fry onion and add to meat. Pour in stock and thicken with cornflour. Season to taste. Cover and cook for 1 hr at 350° Reg 4. Make cobbler by rubbing margarine into flour and salt and mix to a soft dough with the milk. Roll out and cut into eight wedges. Add peas and carrots to meat for last ten minutes. Allow to cool completely and transfer meat mixture to a foil-lined casserole. Lay wedges of cobbler on top. Put dish into a polythene bag and freeze. Casserole may be removed when frozen. Return food to bag.

To Serve.
Remove foil and return rabbit to original casserole with cobbler uppermost. Place into a cold oven set for 350° Reg 4. Heat for 30 min. Raise heat to 425° Reg 7 to cook the cobbler, about 20 min, till golden brown. Serve with boiled potatoes.

Storage time 3 months.   **Freezer space ⅛ cu ft.**

RABBIT PIE

To make 8 portions.

Ingredients.
oil for frying
1 large onion
2 carrots
1 rabbit cut into eight
1 lb neck of lamb or
½ lb stewing steak
1 pt beef stock.

Crust.
6 oz self raising flour
2½ oz lard
½ tsp salt
water to mix.

Chop onion and fry in oil. Remove, and brown rabbit and steak. Put the meat and onions into a large pie dish and add stock and diced carrots. Season. Cover and cook at 350° Reg 4 for 1½ hrs. Make the crust by rubbing fat into flour and salt. Mix to a firm dough with water. Roll out to fit dish in which pie is to be frozen. When meat is completely cold put into foil-lined dishes and lay crust on top. Place in polythene bags and freeze. Dishes may be removed on freezing if required. Return to polythene.

To Serve.
Remove foil from desired amount of pie and return to dish, with crust on top. Place in cold oven set to 350° Reg 4 and heat for 1 hr. Raise heat to 400° Reg 6 to brown crust. Serve with boiled potatoes. Pastry crust can be stored separately, rolled into balls, and put into a polythene bag. In this way sufficient crust can be used for small servings of rabbit.

Storage time 3 months.   **Freezer space ¼ cu ft.**

CURRIED RABBIT

To make 6-8 portions.

Ingredients.

oil for frying	1 tbs chutney
1 rabbit, jointed	2 oz sultanas
2 onions	2 tomatoes
2 tbs curry powder	lemon juice
1 pt stock	seasoning.
1 cooking apple	

Fry rabbit joints in a little oil until browned. Remove from pan and add onions, chopped. When fried, remove also. Add curry powder and stock. Put back the rabbit and onions. Add the chopped apple, the chutney, sultanas, tomatoes, a squeeze of lemon juice and seasoning. Cover and cook for 2 hr. When completely cold put into waxed or foil containers and freeze.

To Serve.

Turn into a pan and heat gently over a low heat. Meanwhile, allowing 2 oz rice per person, boil it in plenty of salted water for 15 min. Drain into colander and rinse with hot water to separate the grains. Pile rice in a border round a serving plate and spoon curry into centre. Serve with one of the following: Dessicated coconut. Raw onion rings. Green salad. Mango chutney. Adjust curry flavouring if it is a little weaker after freezing.

Storage time 3 months.   **Freezer space $\frac{1}{8}$ cu ft.**

VEAL STROGANOFF

To make 4 portions.

Ingredients.

oil for frying
4 veal cutlets
2 onions
2 tsp paprika

1 large tin tomatoes
2 tbs tomato purée
¼ pt soured cream.

Brown the veal in a little oil. Remove cutlets and fry onions in same oil until tender. Add the paprika and cook for 3 min. Stir in the tomatoes, breaking up the fruit, and add tomato purée. Season to taste with salt and black pepper. Return the cutlets and simmer for 1-1½ hr. A little stock may be added if necessary. Thicken with cornflour. Stir in the soured cream gently and do not allow to boil. When completely cold put into a foil-lined casserole or waxed or foil container and freeze.

To Serve.
Return to pan and heat gently until thoroughly hot but do not boil. Serve with noodles. Boil noodles in salted water for 10 min approximately. Drain and put into a hot dish. Drop knobs of butter on top. Alternatively boil 2 oz rice per person in salted water for 15 min. Drain and rinse with hot water and serve immediately. If the veal is heated in the oven in a casserole, creamed, piped potatoes can be browned.

Storage time 3 months.   **Freezer space ⅛ cu ft.**

VEAL GOULASH

To make 6 portions.

Ingredients.

oil for frying	$\frac{3}{4}$ pt water
2 lb veal cut into cubes	2 tbs mild vinegar
3 oz tomato purée	1 tbs cornflour
1 tsp salt	1 tbs paprika
4 small chopped onions	1 tsp caraway seeds.
black pepper	

Cook the onions in a little oil until soft but not brown. Add the tomato purée, paprika, caraway seeds and seasoning. Stir in the veal. Cook gently over a low heat for 5 to 10 min. Add $\frac{3}{4}$ pt water. Simmer until veal is tender for approximately $1\frac{1}{2}$ hr. Mix cornflour in vinegar and stir into gravy to thicken. When completely cold, divide Goulash between two or three foil-lined casseroles according to amounts required. Pack into polythene bags. Secure mouth and freeze. Remove casseroles and return food to bags.

To Serve.

Goulash can be returned to original casserole after removing foil and heated for $1\frac{1}{2}$ hr at 350° Reg 4. Or heat slowly in a covered saucepan. Small dumplings can be added when mixture thaws. Cook for 15 to 20 min.

Dumplings.

Mix 4 oz flour with $1\frac{1}{2}$ oz shredded suet and pinch of salt to a firm dough with water. Mould into 12 balls. Serve with white cabbage and boiled potatoes or rice. Boil rice in plenty of salted water for 15 to 20 min. Rinse with hot water.

Storage time 2 months.   **Freezer space $\frac{1}{4}$ cu ft.**

FRICASSEE OF VEAL

To make 6 portions.

Ingredients.

1½ lb stewing veal	½ pt milk
1 small onion	seasoning.
1 stick celery	
1 small carrot	*For serving:*
bouquet garni	bacon rolls
cornflour	lemon slices
stock	parsley.

Cut the meat into cubes and put with the vegetables, which have been diced, into a pan. Add the bouquet garni and cover with stock. Cook gently until quite tender, approximately 1 hr. Strain off ½ pt stock. Put the meat into a foil-lined casserole and allow to cool. Make a white sauce with the stock and milk, seasoned and thickened with cornflour. When sauce is cold pour over meat and place casserole into a polythene bag and freeze. Bouquet garni must be removed before freezing. Remove casserole when frozen and return food to bag.

To Serve.

Remove foil and return food to original casserole. Heat in a moderate oven 350° Reg 4 for approximately 1½ hr. Serve with creamed potatoes and green vegetable. Garnish with bacon rolls and lemon slices. Crisp fry rashers of streaky bacon and roll. Sprinkle parsley over meat. Potatoes baked in their jackets could accompany this dish.

Storage time 3 months.   **Freezer space ⅛ cu ft.**

VEAL FRICADELLES

To make 4 portions.

Ingredients.

1 lb minced veal	¼ pt water
4 oz suet	seasoning
2 oz minced onion	1 tsp paprika
parsley	½ pt tomato sauce and
1 tsp mixed herbs	2-3 tbs sour cream for
5 oz bread without crusts	serving.
a little milk	

Put bread to soak in milk for ½ hr. Put meat, suet, onion and bread through a fine mincer. Add the water and work in with the hands to absorb water without mix becoming sloppy. Season highly with salt, pepper, herbs and paprika. Roll into small balls on a floured board and fry in hot oil. Freeze without balls touching, on trays. Store in polythene bags when frozen.

To Serve.

Place balls in casserole and pour over sufficient tomato sauce to cover. Cook in oven for 20 min at 35° Reg 4. Stir in sour cream just before serving. Pile Fricadelles on to a serving dish. Garnish with black olives and quarters of lemon.

Other minced meat may be substituted for the veal, but not beef, as the taste is too strong.

Serve with rice or green salad. Allow 2 oz rice per person. Boil in plenty of salted water. Rinse with hot water.

Storage time 2-3 months.   **Freezer space ⅛ cu ft.**

D

HOT WATER CRUST FOR PIES

Sufficient for 1 pie. 8 portions.

12 oz plain flour
1½ tsp salt
4 oz lard

1 beaten egg
½ pt milk.

Place lard and milk into saucepan and bring slowly to the boil. When boiling add flour and salt all at once, and mix quickly using a wooden spoon. Cover with foil, leave to cool. Knead until smooth. Cut off one third and set aside for lid. Knead large piece into ball. Push clenched fist into centre and bring up sides with other hand. Pinching dough to make it thinner and pulling with fingers. Continue until good round shape is achieved. Pleating and pressing out pleats to keep sides smooth. Finished pie should be about 3½ in high and 6 in wide. Keep base small until sides are raised then push it out. Place double thickness of greaseproof paper round pie case and secure with string. Roll out pastry lid. Make hole in centre and decorate with pastry leaves. Put in filling. Put on lid and flute edges. Bake at 400° Reg 6 for ½ hr. Reduce to 350° Reg 4 and bake further hour. Carefully remove paper and brush over with beaten egg. Cook further ½ hr. Leave on baking sheet to cool. Add stock thickened with gelatine, leave for ½ hr then add more stock. When completely cold freeze in polythene bag.

To Serve. Thaw to room temperature approximately 4 hr.

Storage time 3 months. **Freezer space ⅛ cu ft.**

HOT WATER VEAL & HAM PIE FILLINGS

Ingredients.

1½ lb veal in ½ inch cubes   chicken stock cube
½ tsp herbs   1 onion
¾ lb streaky bacon   gelatine
nutmeg   seasoning.

Cut up bacon and mix with onion, veal, herbs, nutmeg and seasoning. Press into raised pastry case. Bake as directed on Page 98. Make stock with chicken stock cube and gelatine. Add stock when cold and freeze in polythene bags.

PORK PIE

Ingredients.

1½ lb pie pork   gelatine
chicken stock cube   seasoning.
1 tbs dried sage and onion
  mix

Mince pork and season well. Mix sage and onion with pork. Press into pastry case and bake as directed. Make stock with chicken stock cube and gelatine. Add stock when cold. The addition of hard boiled eggs is not recommended as they do not freeze well but go rubbery.

GAME PIE

Ingredients.

1½ lb mixed pheasant and   2 rashers bacon.
  rump steak

Mince the meat and cut up bacon into small pieces. Mix together and season. Put into pastry case and bake. Add jellied chicken stock. Freeze.

Storage time 3 months.   **Freezer space ⅛ cu ft.**

VEAL AND BACON PIE

To make 1 pie:—6 portions.

Ingredients.

1 small onion	4 oz streaky bacon
3 peppercorns	8 oz puff pastry
1 tsp mixed herbs	oil to fry
1 lb boneless stewing veal	cornflour
½ pt milk	1 beaten egg.

Slice onion and put into pan with peppercorns, herbs and milk. Bring to the boil, cover and leave aside for 15 min. Strain liquid into jug. Cut veal into cubes and toss in seasoned flour. Cut bacon into small pieces. Fry veal and bacon in oil for 5 min. Pour the strained milk over the meat and bring to the boil. Thicken with cornflour. Line a pie dish with foil allowing foil to stand above rim. When cold pour in the bacon and veal mixture. Roll out the puff pastry and lay across dish. Put pie into polythene bag and freeze. Remove dish when frozen and return pie to bag. Stand pie on edge to conserve space.

To Serve.
Remove foil and return pie to original dish. Place in cold oven set at 400° Reg 6. Bake for 40 min timed from when correct temperature is reached. Crust should be golden brown. Serve with salad, or alternatively, creamed potatoes and garden peas. Test if filling is completely thawed and heated before serving.

Storage time 2 months.   **Freezer space ⅛ cu ft.**

CHICKEN AND BACON PIE

To make 1 pie:—6 portions.

Ingredients.
Filling.

1 medium onion	*Pastry.*
4 chicken joints or	8 oz flour
1 lb chicken pieces	½ tsp salt
1 bay leaf	4 oz mixed margarine/lard
¾ pt chicken stock	1 tsp gelatine.
4 oz streaky bacon	

Place chicken joints in saucepan with sliced onion, bay leaf and stock. Cook for 30 min. Remove chicken from stock. Line base and sides of a 1 lb loaf tin with foil. Cut chicken from bones and put bones back into stock and simmer for 40 min. Remove bay leaf. Cut up bacon. Make pastry by rubbing fat into salt and flour. Mix to a firm dough with water. Roll out two thirds of pastry and line loaf tin. Pack in the chicken meat and bacon. Cover with pastry lid. Cut pastry leaves and make holes in pie. Place leaves round the holes. Brush with beaten egg. Bake pie in hot oven 400° Reg 6 for 35 mins. Leave to cool in the tin. Put ¼ pt of stock into a basin and add gelatine. Place basin in pan of hot water over moderate heat and stir until gelatine dissolves. Cool and pour through holes into pie. Freeze pie when cold and remove from tin when frozen.

To Serve. Allow to thaw and slice. Serve with salad.

Storage time 2 months.   **Freezer space ⅛ cu ft.**

MUSHROOM AND HAM PIE

To make 1 pie:—6 portions.

Ingredients.

4 oz mushrooms	$\frac{3}{4}$ pt stock
1 small green pepper	pinch mixed herbs
1 lb cooked ham	6 oz puff pastry
1 oz margarine	cornflour.

Slice mushrooms. Remove seed from pepper and cut into strips. Boil in a little water for 2 min. Drain and put aside. Cut ham into $\frac{1}{2}$ in dice. Cook mushrooms in a little margarine for 3 min. Add stock and bring to the boil. Thicken with cornflour. Add green pepper and herbs. Put in the ham and simmer for 2 min. Allow to cool. Line a pie-dish with foil leaving it protruding above the rim. When filling completely cold put into the dish. Roll out the puff pastry and lay over dish. Put dish into polythene bag and freeze. When frozen remove dish and return pie to bag. Stand on end to conserve storage space.

To Serve.

Remove foil and return pie to original dish. Put into a cold oven set at 400° Reg 6. Bake for approximately 40 min timed from when correct temperature is reached. Crust should be risen and golden brown. Garnish with hardboiled eggs and serve with chipped potatoes.

Storage time 2 months.   **Freezer space $\frac{1}{8}$ cu ft.**

MINCED BEEF PIE

To make 4 portions.

Ingredients.

Filling.	*Sauce.*
2 lb potatoes	½ pt milk
½ lb carrots	½ lb onions
¾ lb minced beef	1 tbs cornflour
5 oz frozen peas.	2 oz grated cheese for serving.

Make sauce by chopping onions and frying in a little oil until soft. Pour in milk and bring to the boil. Thicken with cornflour and season to taste. Filling:—Slice potatoes and carrots. Fry meat until brown, and season. Mix peas and carrots. Put layers of potatoes, vegetables and meat into a foil-lined casserole and starting and finishing with potatoes. Season and pour sauce over. Cover and cook for 30 min at 375° Reg 5. When completely cold place dish in polythene bag and freeze. Remove dish when frozen.

To Serve.

Remove foil and return to casserole. Place in oven set at 350° Reg 4. When heated through, raise temperature of oven and sprinkle grated cheese over pie. Return to oven without lid and allow cheese topping to brown. This recipe could be made with Savoury Mince very quickly once the mince has thawed. Put the layers of potatoes, vegetables and mince in casserole and add onion sauce and cheese topping. Cook as directed.

Storage time 3 months.   **Freezer space ⅛ cu ft.**

CHICKEN PIE DELUXE

To make 1 pie:—5 portions.

Ingredients.

4 cups chicken pieces	*Pastry.*
½ lb cooked pork sausage	4 oz flour
2 tomatoes	2 oz margarine and lard
10½ oz tin condensed celery	mixed
or asparagus soup	salt
1 tbs milk.	water to mix.

Pour soup into bowl and stir in milk. Add the chicken and sliced sausages. Chop the tomatoes and add. Mix well.
Pastry.
Rub fat into flour and salt and mix to a firm dough with the water. Put filling into a foil-lined pie-dish and cover with round of pastry. Do not cook pie but put dish into a polythene bag and freeze. Dish may be removed when frozen. Return pie to polythene bag.

To Serve.
Remove foil and return pie to original dish. Place in a cold oven set to reach 375° Reg 5. When correct temperature is reached time cooking for 40 min. Raise heat to 400° Reg 6 for last 5 min to brown crust. It is pointless to cook pies which are to be eaten hot before freezing as this uses twice the amount of fuel if the warming time is taken into account. But if the filling has to be cooked, care must be taken to allow this to cool before adding crust. Serve with chipped potatoes.

Storage time 2-3 months.   **Freezer space ⅛ cu ft.**

CORNED BEEF PIE

To make 6 portions.

Ingredients.

6 oz shortcrust pastry   3 lb potatoes
12 oz corned beef   1 pt beef stock.

Peel the potatoes and cut into cubes. Put into a large pan along with the corned beef, also cubed, and the stock. Bring to the boil and simmer until potatoes are soft. Mix the pastry by rubbing 3 oz lard into 6 oz flour with a pinch of salt added. Mix to a firm dough with a little water. Roll out to fit suitable casserole. Line the dish with foil and when potato mixture is cold spoon into dish. Place crust on top and put casserole into a polythene bag. Freeze. Remove casserole when frozen but return food to bag.

To Serve.

Remove foil and return pie to original dish. Place in cold oven set at 350° Reg 4. After allowing time for filling to heat through adjust temperature to 400° Reg 6 to brown crust. Dried peas, previously soaked and boiled, make an ideal vegetable to serve. Boiling a large quantity at one time and dividing them over suitable containers to freeze means they are always available.

Use this recipe for pasties also and freeze with the pastry uncooked.

Storage time 3 months.   **Freezer space $\frac{1}{8}$ cu ft.**

PLOUGHMAN'S PASTY

To make 2 pasties:—4 portions.

Ingredients.

1 lb sausage meat
10 oz tin of condensed
   vegetable soup.

Pastry.

8 oz flour
4 oz mixed margarine and
   lard
½ tsp salt
water to mix.

Mix the vegetable soup with the sausage meat. Make pastry by rubbing fat into flour and salt. Mix to a firm dough with water. Cut in half and roll each piece into a large circle. Divide sausage meat filling over circles and damp edges. Fold over and seal together. Make slits to allow steam to escape. Place on greased baking sheet and bake for 25-30 min at 400° Reg 6 until golden brown. Freeze when completely cold on trays without pasties touching. Put trays in polythene bags. Remove trays when frozen and return pasties to bags. It is recommended that the pasties be cooked before freezing so that they can be eaten cold. They make an ideal picnic or lunch pack.

To Serve.

Allow to thaw to room temperature approximately 2 hr. This process can be hastened by placing pasties in warm oven 350° Reg 4 for 15 min. Serve with potato crisps.

Storage time 2 months.
      Freezer space ⅛ cu ft.

MINCED BEEF AND PARSNIP PASTIES

To make 12 pasties.

Ingredients.

4 medium potatoes	*Pastry.*
2 parsnips	1 lb flour
2 onions	8 oz lard and margarine
1½ lb minced beef	salt
seasoning.	water to mix.

Dice the potatoes and parsnips and chop onions. Cook the vegetables with the minced meat in a little water for 15 min. Add seasoning. Make the pastry by rubbing the fat into the flour and salt and mixing to a firm dough with water. Whilst meat mixture is cooling, roll out the pastry and cut into 12 circles. Divide the meat over each circle and damp edges of pastry. Fold over, sealing edges. Place on floured trays, not touching, and put trays into polythene bags. Freeze. Repack in polythene bags when frozen. If it is intended to eat the pasties cold they may be cooked before freezing. Bake in hot oven 400° Reg 6 for 25-30 min. When cold freeze as above.

To Serve.

Place pasties on to floured trays and put in a cold oven set at 400° Reg 6. Bake for 40 min giving filling time to heat through. Make a gravy with beef stock and thicken with cornflour and serve with the pasties. Peas or spring cabbage are excellent served with these pasties.

Storage time 3 months.   **Freezer space ⅛ cu ft.**

KIDNEY VOL-AU-VENTS

To make 36 cases.

Ingredients.	Filling.
12 oz puff pastry or 36 vol-au-vent cases.	½ lb streaky bacon 1 small onion 4 oz mushrooms cornflour 1½ lb ox kidney.

Roll out the pastry and cut cases by cutting two circles and cutting centre from one. Damp edges and place rim on top of base. Cook cases in hot oven 450° Reg 7 until risen and light brown. Remove rind from bacon and cut into strips. Slice onions and mushrooms. Fry until tender. Cut kidney into small pieces and toss in seasoned flour. Add to bacon and fry for 10 min. Add ½ pt water and boil, stirring well. Cover and simmer for 20 min. Thicken with cornflour. The filling can be packed when cold in waxed containers to be thawed when required. Alternatively, fill cases and freeze on trays. Pack into rigid containers when frozen.

To Serve.
Thaw filling if necessary and fill cases. Heat through in hot oven 400° Reg 6 for 10 min. If cases have been frozen filled set oven to top setting and put vol-au-vents in for 5-6 min to crisp and reheat. A selection of filled and empty cases should be stored for all occasions.

Storage time 3-4 months.   **Freezer space ¼ cu ft.**

FISH ROLLS

To make 15 rolls.

Ingredients.

8 oz tin of tuna, salmon or crab
8 oz short pastry

2 tbs white sauce
1 tsp lemon juice
seasoning.

Make the pastry by rubbing 4 oz mixed, lard and margarine, into 8 oz flour and pinch of salt. Make into a firm dough with water. Roll pastry out into narrow strip similar to preparation for sausage rolls. Make white sauce with milk, seasoning and cornflour and allow to cool. Drain liquor from fish and mix with sauce, lemon juice and seasoning. Spread mixture thickly along one long side of pastry and roll up pastry. Seal up edges by damping. Cut into short lengths and place on trays to be frozen. Remove trays when frozen.

To Serve.
Return rolls to trays, greased and floured, and bake in moderate oven 350° Reg 4 for approximately 10 min. Glaze with beaten egg or milk before cooking. Serve as a supper snack or cut smaller as a party appetiser. Sardines may be used but omit the lemon juice. If preferred, the rolls may be baked before freezing so they can be eaten cold on thawing to room temperature. Fish rolls make an ideal addition to picnic or lunch packs.

Storage time 3 months.   **Freezer space minimal.**

PIZZA

To make 6 Pizza:—6 portions.

Ingredients.

1 lb plain flour	¼ pt water
2 tsp salt	½ oz fresh yeast
½ oz lard	a little oil.

Dissolve yeast in ¼ pt water at blood heat. Leave until frothy. Mix flour and salt and rub in lard. When yeast is ready mix into flour and add sufficient water to make a soft dough. Knead dough until it is smooth and elastic and leaves the sides of the bowl cleanly. Cover with a cloth wrung out in hot water to rise, approximately 1 hr. Turn risen dough on to a floured board and knead a little. Brush with oil and stretch until a large thin sheet is achieved. Cut to fit 6 individual flat baking sheets or place rings on large sheet. Grease well. Brush dough with oil. Pizza bases can be frozen without any fillings. Place waxed paper or foil between layers and place in polythene bag. Freeze.

To Serve.

Take pizza bases and decorate as desired with any of the following. Grated cheese, tomatoes or tomato purée, scrambled egg and bacon strips, sardines and tomato slices, or any combination of these. Sprinkle dried herbs over the top. A glance at the commercially packed herbs will suggest which ones to use according to filling. Bake in a very hot oven 450° Reg 8 for 20-30 min.

Storage time 2 months.   **Freezer space minimal.**

FRUIT PIES

To make 1 pie.

Ingredients for short crust pastry.

6 oz flour   **pinch of salt.**

3 oz fat

Rub the fat into the flour until mixture resembles bread-crumbs and mix to a firm dough with a little water. The fat may be a mixture of lard and margarine or one of the proprietary brands of shortening. Roll out half the pastry and line a shallow dish, having lined the dish with foil. Fill the pastry case with the desired fruit and roll out the remaining pastry to cover. Place in a polythene bag and freeze. The filling may be any of the pre-frozen fruits which can be purchased in bulk. Sprinkle with dry sugar, if required, about 3-4 oz per lb of fruit. Fresh apples do not keep their colour on freezing so it is best to cook with sugar and a little water. When completely cold use to fill the pie. The many tinned fruit fillings one can buy make excellent pies. Use as directed.

To Serve.

Pastry improves with freezing and it would be pointless to pre-bake. Put frozen pie into a cold oven and set for 400° Reg 6. When temperature is reached bake for 20-25 min until golden brown. Serve with hot custard, fresh cream or ice-cream which is always available with a freezer.

Storage time 3 months.   **Freezer space minimal.**

FLAN CASES

SPONGE FLAN CASES FOR SWEET FILLINGS

Ingredients.

3 eggs
3 oz castor sugar

3 oz flour
pinch of salt.

Break eggs into a bowl and add sugar. Whisk by hand or
with a mixer until thick and light. Sift in flour and salt
and fold in gently. Mixture should resemble thick batter.
Pour into greased and floured 8 in flan cases, with raised
base to give correct shape. Bake at 425° Reg 7 for 10 min
until light and springy to touch. Can be made in individual cases. When completely cold, freeze in rigid containers to prevent breaking. Put a layer of greaseproof
paper between flans.

SHORT CRUST PASTRY FOR SAVOURY FILLINGS

Ingredients.

6 oz flour

3 oz lard and margarine,
mixed
pinch salt.

Rub fat into flour and salt and mix to firm dough with
water. Line an 8 in sandwich tin with pastry and cover
with greaseproof paper and layer of butter beans to bake
'blind'. Bake for 15-20 min at 400° Reg 6. Freeze when
cold in rigid containers.

Storage time for flan cases 6 months.

SPONGE FLAN FILLINGS

CHERRY ALMOND

Ingredients.
6 oz cream
14 oz tin cherry fruit filling

few drops almond essence
dessicated coconut.

Whip cream until thick and fold in cherry filling. Stir in almond essence. Spoon into flan case and sprinkle top with the dessicated coconut.

BLACKBERRY

Ingredients.
1 lb dessert blackberries
$\frac{1}{4}$ oz gelatine

$\frac{1}{2}$ pt blackberry juice.

Cook blackberries in a little water with sugar to taste. Simmer until fruit soft but still firm. Pile fruit into flan case. Dissolve the gelatine in the blackberry juice and when almost set pour over the fruit. Decorate with whipped cream.

CHERRY

Ingredients.
$\frac{3}{4}$ lb fresh or tinned cherries   lemon jelly.

Fill flan case with cherries. Remove stones if fresh fruit is used. Cover with lemon jelly on point of setting. Decorate with whipped cream.

SPONGE FLAN FILLINGS

CHOCOLATE PEPPERMINT

Ingredients.

1 pt chocolate blancmange
few drops peppermint
  essence

2 tbs thick cream
6 chocolate peppermint
  creams.

Add peppermint essence to chocolate blancmange. Allow to cool, covering with greaseproof paper to prevent a skin forming. Stir in the cream and spoon into flan case. Cut peppermint creams into halves and decorate flan.

SUNFLOWER PEACH

Ingredients.

16 oz tin peach slices
1 tbs milk
2 tbs custard powder

$\frac{1}{4}$ tsp cinnamon
lemon juice
sugar to taste.

Make peach syrup into $\frac{1}{2}$ pt with milk. Put custard powder into a pan with cinnamon and stir in the syrup. Bring to the boil stirring until it thickens. Simmer for 3 min. Add lemon juice and sugar to taste. Leave to cool then put into flan case. Arrange peach slices radiating from centre with glacé cherry in middle to represent a sunflower.

SPONGE FLAN FILLINGS

CRUNCHY APPLE

Ingredients.

13 oz tin apple filling   1 tbs water
4 oz nut toffee   1 oz cornflakes.

Spoon apple filling into case. Crack toffee and put in pan with water. Melt over low heat. Crush cornflakes and stir into toffee having removed pan from heat. Spread over apple and leave to set for 15 min. Serve with cream.

CHOCOLATE APRICOT WHIP

Ingredients.

½ pt thick custard   1 oz coarsely grated
14½ oz tin apricot filling   chocolate

Whisk apricot into cooled custard and fold in half the chocolate. Spoon into flan case and sprinkle remaining chocolate over top. Serve alone.

FRESH FRUIT FILLINGS

Spread the inside of large or individual flans with jam and fill with fresh fruit, e.g. strawberries, raspberries, cherries. Decorate with piped cream. Or fruit may be set in a jelly if desired. There is an excellent commercial preparation on the market for this purpose but if jelly is used it must be made with less water.

MERINGUE TOPPED FLANS

MERINGUE

Ingredients.
3 egg whites   **6 oz castor sugar.**
pinch of salt

Add pinch of salt to egg whites and beat until stiff:—the mixture should stand in peaks. Fold the sugar in lightly using a metal spoon. Fill the flan cases with desired filling and spread meringue over, leaving a rough finish. Bake in a hot oven 425° Reg 7 until meringue is crisp and lightly browned.

FRUIT MERINGUE

Ingredients.
1 tin of fruit as desired   **meringue topping.**

Fill flan case with fruit, omit juice. Any tinned variety without stones will do. Spread meringue over fruit and bake in a hot oven 425° Reg 7 until crisp and brown. Serve immediately for best results.

ICE SURPRISE

Ingredients.
sufficient vanilla ice cream   **meringue topping.**

Lay vanilla ice cream in base of flan case. Have meringue ready and spread quickly over ice cream. Put in hot oven 450° Reg 8 for 5 min. Serve immediately. Other flavours of ice cream could be used or fruit added with the ice cream.

SHORT CRUST FLAN FILLINGS

BACON AND CORN

Ingredients.

8 oz cooked bacon

2 eggs

¼ pt milk

7 oz tin sweet corn

3 extra rashers streaky bacon.

Cut fat from cold bacon and cut into ½ in cubes. Beat eggs and milk together. Drain liquid from corn and add corn to eggs. Stir in cooked bacon and pepper to taste. Cut bacon rashers in half and roll. Put corn mixture into flan and stand bacon rolls round edge. Bake in oven at 375° Reg 5 for 40 min until firm.

EGG AND CHEESE

Ingredients.

3 eggs

3 oz grated cheese

tomato slices

seasoning

few cooked mushrooms.

Beat eggs and add cheese. Season to taste. Spoon into case and place tomato rings on top. Bake in oven at 375° Reg 5 for 30 min. Garnish with cooked mushrooms. Both these flans may be served with salad or potato crisps or the commercially prepared maize sticks.

SHORT CRUST FLAN FILLINGS

CORN AND CHEESE

Ingredients.

3 rashers streaky bacon
2 eggs
2 tbs milk
1 oz grated cheddar cheese

$\frac{1}{2}$ tsp salt
black pepper
$10\frac{1}{2}$ oz tin sweet corn.

Remove rind from bacon and cut into strips. Beat eggs with salt, milk and black pepper. Add corn and cheese. Mix well. Pour into flan case and arrange bacon on top. Bake in oven for 30-35 min at 375° Reg 5. Serve hot with salad. Approximately 3 oz of grated cheese can be added to the pastry mix for fillings like this if desired.

CHICKEN AND VEGETABLE

Ingredients.

6 oz frozen peas and carrots
10 oz cooked chicken meat
3 rashers streaky bacon

2 eggs
$\frac{1}{4}$ pt milk.

Cook vegetables for 5 min in a little water. Cut chicken into dice and bacon rashers in half. Place chicken in case then vegetables. Beat eggs into milk and season. Pour into flan. Arrange bacon on top. Bake for 30 min at 375° Reg 5. Serve with salad or chipped potatoes.

QUICHE LORRAINE

To make 1 flan.

Ingredients.

4 oz shortcrust pastry	2 eggs
½ oz margarine	2 oz grated cheese
1 onion	¼ pt milk or thin cream.
1 oz bacon	

Make the pastry by rubbing 2 oz lard and margarine into 4 oz flour. Add pinch of salt. Roll out and line a flan case or sponge tin. First line with foil unless the case may be left in freezer. Fry onion in margarine until tender and add bacon. Fry until margarine is golden brown. Pour mixture into pastry case. Beat the eggs, cheese and milk and season with pepper. Pour into flan case. Bake in moderately hot oven 375° Reg 5 for 30 min. Cool completely before freezing. Once frozen the flan case may be removed.

To Serve.

Allow to thaw to room temperature and serve cold with a green salad or reheat in moderate oven 350° Reg 4 for 20 min. Individual Quiche Lorraine can be made for lunch packs. The filling may be varied to suit individual taste. Sausage, onion and eggs. Cheese and egg. Chives give a more delicate flavour than the onion if desired.

Storage time 2 months.   **Freezer space minimal.**

GINGERBREAD PEAR PUDDING

To make 1 pudding:—6 portions.

Ingredients.

2 oz margarine
2 oz golden syrup and
  black treacle mixed
6 tbs milk
$\frac{1}{2}$ tsp bicarbonate soda
1 beaten egg

5 oz flour
1-2 tsp ground ginger
$\frac{1}{4}$ tsp mixed spice
2 oz soft brown sugar
tin of pear halves for
  serving.

Stir margarine, brown sugar and syrup in saucepan over a low heat until dissolved. Cool slightly. Dissolve bicarbonate soda in 1 tbs milk. Add the rest of the milk to sugar mixture. Stir in the dry ingredients and the egg and beat until smooth. Stir in bicarbonate soda. Pour sponge mixture into waxed or foil container and freeze.

To Serve.

Grease a pudding basin and place pear halves in bottom. Turn out gingerbread mixture on to the pears. Cover basin with greaseproof paper and tie with fine string. Place pudding in a pan with sufficient water to rise half way up the basin. Steam for 2 hr checking that water remains at correct level. Serve with custard or single cream. These quantities may be increased as desired. It is better to freeze the uncooked mixture as reheating would use almost as much fuel. Fresh pears may be used but a little sugar and water should be poured over before adding sponge.

Storage time 2 months.   **Freezer space minimal.**

APPLE AND RASPBERRY PIE

To make 1 pie:—6 portions.

Ingredients.

Pastry.	*Filling.*
4 oz margarine	3-4 tbs raspberry jam
7 oz flour	1 lb cooking apples
1 oz sugar	1 oz sugar.
1 egg	
3 tsb milk.	

Rub fat into flour and sugar, mix in egg and milk to make a firm soft dough. Knead a little. Roll out two thirds of pastry and line a pudding basin which has already been lined with foil. Allow foil to project above basin. Spoon jam into base. Slice apples thinly and cook in a little water with the sugar. When cold pour into basin. Cover fruit with remaining pastry. Place basin inside a polythene bag and freeze. Basin can be removed on freezing but return pudding to bag.

To Serve.

Remove foil and return pudding to original basin. Cover pudding with greaseproof paper and tie in usual manner. Place in a pan of cold water sufficient to reach half way up the basin. Steam pudding for 2 hr. Checking that it does not boil dry. Turn out on to a hot serving dish and serve with custard. Using 3 oz suet and 2 oz sugar with 8 oz flour the casing could be made of suet crust.

Storage time 6 months.   **Freezer space $\frac{1}{8}$ cu ft.**

ORANGE PUDDING

To make 1 pudding:—6 portions.

Ingredients.

4 oz margarine
4 oz sugar
2 eggs
6 oz S.R. flour

tin mandarin oranges for
   serving
arrowroot for serving.

To make sponge.
Cream margarine and sugar together. Beat in eggs, adding a little flour with each to prevent curdling. Fold in remaining flour. Turn into foil or waxed containers or polythene bags. This sponge can be made in large quantities and frozen to use as a base for various flavoured puddings. If individual containers are used each member of the family could have his choice.

To Serve.
Grease a pudding basin and place mandarin oranges in bottom. Turn out sufficient sponge mix, still frozen, on top of fruit. Place pudding in cold oven at 375° Reg 5 for 30 min. Timed from temperature being reached. Or steam in pan of boiling water sufficient to come halfway up the basin, for 1¼ hr. Turn out on to a shallow dish so that fruit is uppermost. Serve with a sauce made from the orange juice thickened with arrowroot and a little added sugar.

Storage time 2 months.   **Freezer space minimal.**

PINEAPPLE UPSIDE-DOWN PUDDING

To make 1 pudding:—6 portions.

Ingredients.

Sponge mixture.
4 oz margarine
4 oz sugar
3 eggs
6 oz S.R. flour.

Topping (for serving).
1 tin drained pineapple
  rings
3 tbs juice
½ oz glacé cherries
2 oz demerara sugar.

To make sponge.
Cream the margarine and sugar. Beat in the eggs adding a little flour with each one to prevent curdling. Fold in remaining flour. These quantities may be doubled or trebled as desired. Divide mixture over suitably sized, waxed or foil containers, or spoon into polythene bags. Freeze.

To Serve.
Place pineapple juice and sugar in an oven proof dish or basin. Arrange pineapple rings with cherries in the holes on base of dish. Turn out the required amount of sponge-mix on to the fruit. This is easier if done while still frozen. Pudding may be put directly into a cold oven. Set oven to reach 375° Reg 5. The sponge mixture will thaw as this temperature is reached. Then cook pudding for 30 min until it is risen and turning slightly golden. Turn out on to a dish so that fruit is uppermost. Serve with single cream (to pour over) or a spoonful of whipped double-cream on each portion.

Storage time 2 months.   **Freezer space minimal.**

CHOCOLATE CUPS

To make 8 portions.

Ingredients.

1 large can evaporated milk
1 tsp vanilla essence
4 tbs cornflour
2 tbs castor sugar

8 oz plain chocolate
1 egg yolk
1 oz butter.

Make the evaporated milk into $1\frac{1}{2}$ pt with water and stir in the vanilla essence. Mix the cornflour and sugar to a smooth paste with 4 tbs of the 'milk'. Heat the remainder of the 'milk' until almost boiling then pour into the cornflour and stir. Pour into another pan and bring to the boil stirring well. Cook for 3 min. Melt the chocolate over hot water and add to the 'milk' and cornflour along with the egg yolk. Beat until smooth. Cool slightly and then add the melted butter. Pour into waxed containers and allow to cool completely before freezing.

To Serve.
This makes a delightful sweet for summer evenings. Allow to thaw and serve with ice cream or whipped cream. The flavouring can be varied by the use of coffee essence or mashed soft fruits, e.g. strawberries or raspberries. Bananas will not freeze but must be served directly.

Storage time 2 months.　　　　　**Freezer space minimal.**

PANCAKES

To make 6-8 pancakes.

Ingredients.

oil for frying
4 oz flour
¼ tsp salt

1 egg
½ pt milk.

Make a well in centre of salt and flour mix, and add egg. Beat in flour and add milk gradually. Beat for 5-10 min. Allow to stand, then stir before cooking. Heat a little oil in frying pan and pour in sufficient batter to thinly coat pan. Cook until golden brown, turn over and cook other side. When cold place between layers of foil and freeze in polythene.

To Serve.
Reheat pancakes in hot oven 375° Reg 5. Serve with sugar and lemon or stuff with savoury or sweet fillings.

Sweet Fillings. Jam and thick cream. Stewed fruit. Mince-meat.

Savoury Fillings. Cream cheese and chopped chives. Cooked chopped ham. Grilled mushrooms. Savoury Mince. Shrimps cooked in butter.

If the pancakes are filled and rolled they can be served with an appropriate sauce poured over. The fillings can be added before warming, placing two or more compatible fillings between pancake layers. The whole to be topped with fruit or savoury sauce as required.

Storage time 2 months. **Freezer space minimal.**

ICE CREAM

VANILLA ICE

To make 1 pint.

Ingredients.
1 pt thin cream
3 oz sugar

1 vanilla pod
pinch of salt.

Put cream and vanilla pod into a pan and bring almost to the boil. Reduce heat and stir in the sugar and a pinch of salt. Allow to cool and remove vanilla pod. Pour mixture into a rigid plastic container and freeze until mushy. Take from freezer and beat, either by hand or with an electric beater. Freeze for a further 2 hr beating once again during this time. Ice cream may now be transferred to normal storage part of the freezer.

FLAVOURED ICE

To make 1 pint.

Ingredients.
¾ pt double cream
½ pt fruit purée

1½ tbs castor sugar.

Beat the cream until quite thick and stir in the fruit purée and the sugar. Pour into rigid plastic container and freeze without stirring.

To Serve Ice Cream.
Remove from freezer a short while before it is required.

Storage time 3 months.   **Freezer space minimal.**

SCONES

To make 20 scones.

Ingredients.

1½ lb flour	8 oz sugar
8 oz margarine	3 oz sultanas.

Rub fat into flour and sugar and mix in the sultanas. Mix to a firm dough with water. With floured hands mould into small cakes and place on a greased and floured baking sheet. Bake in a moderately hot oven 375° Reg 5 for approximately 15 min until risen and golden brown. This is not the traditional scone mix but rather richer. It is one which I find gives excellent results and there seems little point in using freezer space to store inferior food. When completely cold store in polythene bags and freeze.

To Serve.

Remove just the quantity needed and allow to thaw to room temperature. This can be speeded by placing in a hot oven for 5 min.

The fruit may be varied using cherries, dates or currants in place of the sultanas.

Plain scones without any fruit are delicious served with jam and cream.

Oatmeal Scones. Use ½ lb fine oatmeal in place of the same amount of flour for a rich oaty scone.

Storage time 6 months.   **Freezer space minimal.**

CHEESE SCONES

To make 12 scones.

Ingredients.

1 lb self raising flour
2 oz butter
pinch of salt

pinch dry mustard
4 oz grated cheddar cheese
milk to mix.

Sieve flour, salt and mustard into a bowl. Rub in the butter until mixture resembles breadcrumbs. Add almost all the cheese. Mix to a soft dough with milk. Turn on to a floured board and roll out to a round $\frac{1}{2}$ in thick. Cut into 12 scones. Brush with milk and sprinkle over the rest of the cheese. Bake in a hot oven 425° Reg 7 for 8-10 min until slightly brown. When completely cold pack into polythene bags and freeze.

To Serve.
Allow to thaw to room temperature and slice through. A light covering of butter can be added if wished. Delicious served with watercress. Scones can be popped into a hot oven for a few minutes to aid thawing, and buttered while still warm. Always cook cakes before freezing as nothing is really gained by freezing uncooked. Small cakes thaw quite quickly and are ready then when needed. Double or treble quantities as desired.

Storage time 6 months.

Freezer space $\frac{1}{8}$ cu ft.

ALMOND SLICES

To make 16 slices.

Ingredients.
Short Crust Pastry.

6 oz flour
3 oz fat
pinch of salt
raspberry jam
water to mix.

Filling.
3 oz margarine
3 oz sugar
4 oz flour
almond essence
1 egg.

Make pastry by rubbing fat into flour and salt and mixing to a firm dough with a little water. Line patty tins or a large rectangular shallow tin. Spread raspberry jam on base and add almond mixture. Cream fat and sugar together and beat in egg. Fold in flour and enough milk to give a dropping consistency. Stir in a few drops of almond essence. Pour mixture over jam and bake in moderately hot oven 400° Reg 6 for 20 min.

Glacé cherries and split almonds can replace the jam and almond essence. Pour the sponge mixture over a layer of cherries and almonds in the pastry case. When completely cold slice into fingers and pack in a rigid container to freeze.

To Serve.
Allow the almond slices to thaw to room temperature approximately 30 min. Pastry becomes brittle on freezing so it is better to store in something which will protect it.

Storage time 3 months.   **Freezer space ⅛ cu ft.**

E

SMALL BATCH CAKES

To make 24 buns.

Ingredients.

8 oz butter or margarine
8 oz sugar
4 eggs

8 oz flour
1 tsp baking powder.

Cream fat and sugar and add eggs gradually, beating well. Fold in flour and baking powder and add milk if necessary. Mixture must be of dropping consistency. Spoon the mixture into patty tins or paper cake cases. Bake at 400° Reg 6 for 15 mins until risen and golden. Allow to cool and put into polythene bags to freeze.

This mixture may be varied by the addition of fruit such as cherries, sultanas or currants. Or by adding cocoa for chocolate buns. (In this case flour equal to the amounts of cocoa must be omitted.)

Iced buns do not keep their quality as long as plain ones so it is better to ice after removing from freezer. But if freezing, then freeze unwrapped until icing has set. Then wrap and put into boxes to protect the icing.

To Serve.

Unwrap iced cakes before thawing. Allow plain cakes to thaw to room temperature approximately 1-2 hr. Decoration can be done before thawing is completed.

Storage time 6 months, uniced.   **Freezer space $\frac{1}{8}$ cu ft.**

CHOCOLATE SANDWICH CAKE

To make 1 cake.

Ingredients.

3 oz margarine
3 oz castor sugar
2 eggs

3 oz self raising flour
1 tbs cocoa.

Cream fat and sugar and beat in eggs. Fold in flour and cocoa and add a little milk if necessary to achieve dropping consistency. Spoon into a greased and floured cake tin or two sandwich tins and bake large cake for 45 min at 350° Reg 4 or small cakes at 375° Reg 5 for 25-30 min. Pack in polythene and freeze when cold.

To Serve.
Allow to thaw to room temperature until the large cake can be cut through. Sandwich together with chocolate butter-cream.

BUTTER CREAM

Ingredients.
4 oz butter or margarine   6 oz icing sugar.

Cream fat and sugar until soft and add a few drops of vanilla essence.

Chocolate butter cream:—replace 1 tbs sugar with cocoa.

Coffee butter cream:—omit vanilla essence and add coffee. The cream can be made and frozen separately in waxed containers.

Storage time 6 months without filling.

VICTORIA SANDWICH CAKE

To make 1 sandwich.

Ingredients.

4 oz butter or margarine	**4 oz flour**
4 oz sugar	**½ tsp baking powder.**
2 eggs	

Cream fat and sugar till creamy. Beat in eggs. Fold in the flour and baking powder and add a little milk if necessary to achieve dropping consistency. Put into two greased and floured sandwich tins and bake in moderate oven 375° Reg 5 for 25-30 min. Cool on wire tray. When cold, place waxed paper between layers and put into polythene bag to freeze.

To Serve.

Allow sandwich cakes to thaw to room temperature about 3-4 hr. Sandwich together with jam, or cream and dust with castor sugar.

Sandwich cakes may be filled with butter cream before freezing but remember once sandwiched together they take longer to thaw.

Icing also can be done before freezing but this reduces the storage time. As decoration can be done while cake is thawing nothing is really gained. And on no account must they be layered with jam before freezing.

Storage time 6 months.   **Freezer space minimal.**

SHORTBREAD

To make 8 pieces.

Ingredients.

5 oz flour	2 oz castor sugar
1 oz rice flour	4 oz butter.

Sieve flour and sugar into a bowl and add rice flour. Rub in the butter and knead mixture together. Press into a lined baking tin and prick with a fork. Bake in a moderate oven 350° Reg 4 for approximately 1 hr until firm and golden brown. Cool on a wire tray. Dredge with castor sugar and cut into wedges. Pack into rigid container and freeze.

GINGER SHORTBREAD

To make 8 pieces.

Ingredients.

6 oz flour	4 oz butter
2 oz castor sugar	1 oz chopped crystallized
$\frac{1}{2}$-1 tsp ground ginger	ginger.

Rub butter into dry ingredients and add chopped ginger. Knead mixture and press into lined baking tin. Prick with fork. Bake in moderate oven 350° Reg 4 until firm and golden brown, approximately 1 hr. Leave in tin to cool. Pack into rigid container to freeze.

To Serve. Allow shortbreads to thaw to room temperature

Storage time 6 months.   **Freezer space minimal.**

CRUNCHIES

To make 16 biscuits.

Ingredients.

4 cups rolled oats	1½ cups sugar
2 cups plain flour	2 cups coconut
2 tsp bicarb soda	8 oz margarine.
4 tbs syrup	

Melt syrup and margarine in a pan and add bicarb. Take off the heat and beat to a froth. Mix rest of dry ingredients together and add to syrup. If very dry add a little milk. Press into a greased shallow baking tin and bake in a moderate oven 350° Reg 4 for about 30 min. When cool cut into squares. When completely cold pack into a polythene bag and freeze.

To Serve.

Allow crunchies to thaw to room temperature in the bags approximately 2 hr.

DATE CRUNCHIES

Additional ingredients.

6 oz chopped dates   **grated rind of lemon.**

Put dates, lemon rind and a little water into pan. Heat until soft. Put half crunchie mixture into baking tin and cover with dates. Put remainder of mixture on top. Bake.

Storage time 6 months.   **Freezer space minimal.**

BOILED DATE LOAF

To make 1 loaf.

Ingredients.

6 oz brown sugar	3 oz chopped dates
1 third pt milk	4 oz margarine
3 oz sultanas	10 oz flour.
1 egg.	

Put sugar, milk, sultanas, dates and margarine into a pan and heat gently to boiling point. Put aside to cool. Beat an egg and add to the tepid mixture with the flour. Pour into a greased loaf tin and bake in a moderate oven 350° Reg 4 for 1 hr. When completely cold put into a polythene bag and freeze.

CURRANT LOAF

To make 2 loaves.

Ingredients.

1 lb flour	1 lb currants
8 oz margarine	1 tsp spice
8 oz sugar	3 eggs.

Rub the margarine into the flour and spice and stir in sugar and fruit. Beat the eggs and fold into mixture. Put into greased loaf tins and bake for 1½ hr at 350° Reg 4.

Storage time 4 months. **Freezer space ⅛ cu ft.**

ECCLES CAKES

To make 12 cakes.

Ingredients.

6 oz frozen puff pastry	1 tbs sugar
3 tbs currants	½ tsp mixed spice
½ oz butter	sugar for topping.

Roll out the pastry thinly as soon as it has thawed enough. Cut into four rounds. Cream the butter and sugar and stir in the currants. Put a teaspoonful of the mixture into each round of pastry and sprinkle over a little spice. Bring the edges of the pastry together to form a top and turn the cake over. Roll out. Make two cuts in the top of cake. Brush with milk and sprinkle with sugar. Place on a greased tray and bake for 20 min in a hot oven 425° Reg 7. Allow to cool completely and freeze without covering to prevent the cakes sticking together. Store in containers.

To Serve.
Allow Eccles cakes to reach room temperature. If they are a little 'sad' because of freezing then pop into a hot oven for a few minutes. Alternatively, the Eccles cakes may be frozen uncooked and baked when required. Various mixtures of fruit may be used in place of the currants. Served hot with custard they make an easy sweet course.

Storage time 3 months.   **Freezer space minimal.**

BREAD

To make 12 1 lb loaves.

Ingredients.

6 lb strong plain white flour
4 tbs sugar

4 oz fresh yeast or 2 oz
    dried yeast
3 tbs salt.

Put tins and flour to warm in cool oven. Break yeast into basin, add sugar and cream together. Mix $\frac{1}{2}$ pt boiling and $\frac{1}{2}$ pt cold water, pour over yeast. Grease and flour tins. Pour flour into bowl. Add $\frac{1}{2}$ pt boiling and $\frac{1}{2}$ pt cold water to salt. Empty yeast and salt water into flour. With a further $\frac{3}{4}$ pt mixed water, mix to a firm dough which leaves sides of bowl cleanly. Knead. Put to rise, covered by a damp cloth. When risen, turn on to floured surface and knead. Cut into pieces to fill tins up to halfway. Cover again and leave to rise approximately 1 hr until twice size. This dough can be put, covered into the fridge to retard rising for convenience. The retarded dough will finish rising in the kitchen while the oven heats to the required 450° Reg 8. Bake for 30 min. Rapping sharply on the bottom should produce a hollow sound when baked. The unbaked dough may be put into the freezer, but storing of baked bread is more convenient. When cool, wrap in polythene bags and freeze. Bread thaws naturally in about 4 hr. But loaves may be wrapped in foil and put into a hot oven for 10 min to speed the process.

Storage time 1 month.　　　　　　**Freezer space 1 cu ft.**

SULTANA TEACAKES

To make 15 teacakes.

Ingredients.

12 oz flour
¼ tsp salt
½ oz fresh yeast or ¼ oz
   dried yeast
1 tbs sugar

⅓ pt milk and water
1 egg
1 oz margarine
3 oz sultanas.

Warm the milk and water until tepid. Cream the yeast and sugar and stir in the liquid. Put the flour, salt and sultanas into a bowl and rub in the margarine. Make a well and pour in the yeast mixture. Add the beaten egg and mix into a soft dough. Knead until dough leaves sides of bowl cleanly. Put aside to rise to twice size. When risen, cut into pieces and shape into small cakes, kneading a little as necessary. Place on a greased and floured baking tray and leave to rise again. Bake in a hot oven 450° Reg 8 for 15-20 min. Before completely cooked take from oven and brush with a little beaten egg. When completely cold put into polythene bags to freeze.

To Serve.

Allow teacakes to thaw to room temperature, split and spread with butter. With the addition of ½ tsp of mixed spice and 1 oz of candied peel this recipe makes Hot Cross Buns. Cut a cross on the buns before baking. When baked glaze with milk and sugar.

Storage time 6 months.   **Freezer space ⅛ cu ft.**

IRISH SODA BREAD

To make four cobs.

Ingredients.

2 lb flour	2 tsp bicarbonate of soda
1 tsp salt	2 oz lard
2 tsp cream of tartar	1 pt milk.

Rub the fat into the other dry ingredients. Stir enough milk into centre to make a soft spongy dough. Turn on to a floured board and knead. Cut into four pieces and shape into rounds about 2 in thick. Flour a baking sheet and put the cobs on to this. Make three lines on top of each. Bake in a moderately hot oven 400° Reg 6 for 35 min. The cobs should rise well while cooking. Allow to cool completely and wrap in foil before putting into polythene bags. Freeze.

To Serve.

This soda bread is best served warm so put the foil wrapped cobs into hot oven to thaw and warm. Unwrap foil and leave for steam to escape before cutting.

Made into smaller rolls or cobs this would prove excellent for breakfast rolls or dinner cobs. Alternatively use for Hamburgers. Put the hamburger between a sliced roll while still warm.

Storage time 1 month.   **Freezer space ⅛ cu ft.**

FRENCH ROLLS

To make 20 rolls.

Ingredients.

1 oz fresh yeast or ½ oz
   dried yeast
1 heaped tsp salt
1 level tsp sugar

2 oz margarine
14 oz milk and water mixed
1½ lb strong plain flour.

Bring milk and water to 110°. Stir in the yeast. Sieve flour into large bowl and add salt and sugar. Rub in the margarine. Pour in yeast mixture and mix well with a wooden spoon. When dough leaves sides of bowl cleanly turn on to a floured board and knead. When dough is smooth put to rise under a cloth wrung out in hot water. When risen to twice size, knead again. Divide dough into smooth rolls and put on to floured baking sheet to rise. Cover with cloth. When risen make diagonal cuts in dough and brush with milk. Rolls may be frozen unbaked but time must be allowed for dough to recover on taking from freezer to bake. It is more convenient to bake before freezing. Bake in hot oven 425° Reg 7 for 15-20 min. Cool and put into polythene bags to freeze.

To Serve. Allow rolls to thaw to room temperature and serve with butter. The process may be hastened by popping the rolls into a hot oven for 5-8 min.

Storage time 1 month.   **Freezer space ¼ cu ft.**

OAT CAKES

To make 12 cakes.

Ingredients.

8 oz fine oatmeal
4 oz plain flour
1 tsp salt

½ oz fresh yeast or ¼ oz
    dried yeast
¼ pt tepid water
½ pt milk.

Mix the dry ingredients together. Cream the yeast with the tepid water. Slowly add the yeast mixture to the dry mixture and then the milk to make a batter. Allow this batter to stand in a warm place for ½ hr. Ideally the oat cakes should be cooked on a griddle but a large frying pan or the solid hot-plate of the earlier type of electric cooker will serve equally well. Grease the surface to be used and drop spoonfuls of the mixture on when it is hot. When the top surface sets then turn over to cook the other side. Allow to cool and store in rigid containers with foil between the layers. Freeze.

To Serve.

Reheat the oat cakes in hot oven 400° Reg 6 for 5-8 min. Serve hot with butter. Or to allow to reach room temperature and spread with butter or savoury topping. These may also be fried alongside the breakfast bacon and served hot. Serve with soup or salad for a lunch snack.

Storage time 5 months.   **Freezer space minimal.**

RISOTTO

To make 6 portions.

Ingredients.

12 oz long grain rice	2 pts chicken stock
1 onion	seasoning
2 oz margarine or oil	3 oz grated cheese (half used for serving).

Chop the onion finely and fry in some of the oil but do not brown. Put in the dry rice and stir well. Add the stock gradually as it is absorbed, letting the rice cook gently. Stir occasionally. This should take about 30 min. Do not allow rice to become sticky. Season to taste and stir in half the grated cheese. When completely cold freeze. This makes a basic risotto to which various ingredients may be added on thawing. A drier risotto can be achieved by using cooked rice. Fry the onion and add the cooked rice and any meats, etc. Only a very little stock is then necessary. A supply of cooked rice may be kept in polythene bags in the freezer.

To Serve.

Return risotto to pan and reheat gently, stirring occasionally. A selection of meat, fish or vegetables may be added. Alternatively, heat risotto in a casserole in a warm oven 300° Reg 2. Serve with grated cheese.

Storage time 3 months.   **Freezer space $\frac{1}{8}$ cu ft.**

RISOTTO VARIATIONS

To make 6 portions.

Ingredients.	*Variations.*
12 oz rice	peas, diced ham
1 onion	tomatoes
2 oz margarine or oil	mushrooms
2 pts chicken stock	shellfish
seasoning	cooked meat
3 oz grated cheese.	cooked fowl.

Make plain risotto by frying onion and rice in stock, or using previously cooked rice and frying in oil. Add meats, vegetables or fish as desired and heat through. Season and allow to cool. This mixture can be frozen as with the plain risotto but it is quick to make if the rice is pre-cooked and the freezer space could be put to better use. However, left-over rice from other meals can be frozen and used in this way to advantage. Chicken livers add a particularly good flavour to risotto.

To Serve.
Return to pan, if taken from freezer, and reheat slowly over a low heat, stirring occasionally. Although rice dishes freeze well and reheat successfully it is advisable to serve immediately as they deteriorate if an attempt is made to keep them warm. Risotto is an ideal dish for a buffet party, needing little time to prepare. Serve with a side dish of grated cheese.

Storage time 3 months. **Freezer space $\frac{1}{8}$ cu ft.**

NASI GORENG

To make 6 portions.

Ingredients.
4 oz cooked ham
4 oz cooked chicken
4 oz cooked liver
4 oz salami
1 onion
1 glove garlic
4 oz prawns
½ tsp ground coriander
1 tbs soy sauce

Garnish (for serving).
2 eggs
shredded lettuce
tomato slices
cucumber strips
12oz cooked, cold rice.

Dice the cooked ham and cut the chicken, liver and salami into strips. Chop the onion and fry in 3 tbs oil until tender. Do not brown. Remove and gently fry crushed garlic in same oil. Add coriander and the meat and sauté. Add the onion and the cooked rice. Cook for approximately 15 min tossing regularly to ensure even cooking. Add the prawns and soy sauce, cook for a further 5 min. When completely cold, turn into waxed or foil container and freeze.

To Serve.
Empty rice mixture into a casserole and reheat in a slow oven 300° Reg 2 for approximately 1½ hr. Meanwhile make a flat omelette with the two eggs and when cold cut into strips. Pile mixture on to a large dish and lay omelette across the top. Garnish with lettuce, tomato and cucumber.

Storage time 3 months.   **Freezer space ⅛ cu ft.**

EVER READY POTATOES

CHIPPED POTATOES

Prepare chips as usual and fry in deep, hot fat until tender but not browned. Drain on kitchen paper, changing paper to absorb most of fat. When completely cold, pack into polythene bags and freeze.

Chips may be blanched instead of cooking in fat. Drain and open freeze on trays before packing or the chips will stick together on freezing.

To Serve.
Reheat the cooked chips while still frozen in deep hot fat. The blanched chips will require longer cooking time but this should be done while frozen.

Storage time 3 months.   **Freezer space minimal.**

DUCHESS POTATOES

Ingredients.
2 lb sliced potatoes	**1 egg**
2 oz butter	**seasoning.**

Boil potatoes in salted water and mash well. Beat in the butter and egg. Season to taste. Pipe the mixture on to foil-lined trays and freeze without covering. When frozen pack into containers.

To Serve.
Put Duchess Potatoes on to greased baking sheet while still frozen and brush with milk or beaten egg. Brown in moderately hot oven 400° Reg 6 for 25 min.

Storage time 3 months.   **Freezer space $\frac{1}{8}$ cu ft.**

CHICKEN AND CHEESE CROQUETTES

To make 4 portions.

Ingredients.

10 oz cooked chicken
1 onion
1 oz margarine
1 oz flour

$\frac{1}{4}$ pt chicken stock
2 oz grated cheese
breadcrumbs
seasoning
1 egg.

Put the chicken and onion through a fine mincer or blender. Melt margarine in a pan and stir in the flour. Stir rapidly without cooking until mixture forms a ball. Add the minced meat and onion and cheese, stirring in the stock as required. Season well. Allow to cool and form into rolls. Coat with egg and breadcrumbs. Place on trays without rolls touching, put trays in polythene bags to freeze. Trays may be removed when frozen and rolls returned to bags.

To Serve.

Fry croquettes in hot fat turning occasionally, until golden brown. Or fry in deep fat. Chicken Croquettes are excellent served with green salad for a light supper. Alternatively, serve with chipped potatoes and green vegetable for a more satisfying meal. If the Croquettes are made rather smaller they make excellent 'bites' for a party.

Storage time 3 months.   **Freezer space minimal.**

CHEESE AND BACON CROQUETTES

To make 16 croquettes.

Ingredients.

8 rashers bacon	$\frac{1}{4}$ tsp dry mustard
$\frac{1}{2}$ lb cold mashed potatoes	8 oz breadcrumbs
8 oz grated cheddar cheese	2 eggs and 2 tbs water.

Cut bacon into strips and fry. Mix bacon, fat, cheese, mustard and pinch of pepper into potatoes. Divide into 16 pieces and shape into croquettes on a floured board. Beat eggs and water in a shallow dish. Spread breadcrumbs on greaseproof paper. Dip each croquette in egg and then breadcrumbs. Pack between layers of foil or greaseproof paper and freeze on flat trays to keep separate. When frozen pack into polythene bags or rigid containers.

To Serve.

Fry croquettes in deep fat in chip-pan basket for four to six minutes until golden brown. Or fry in shallow fat, turning to brown both sides, for seven or eight minutes. Drain on kitchen paper before serving. Keep hot. Serve with sliced tomato and watercress. For a substantial snack for the children serve with baked beans. Freeze uncooked as no saving in either time or fuel is achieved by cooking first.

Storage time 2 months.   **Freezer space $\frac{1}{8}$ cu ft.**

HAM AND CHICKEN CROQUETTES

To make 16 croquettes.

Ingredients.

2 oz margarine	2 lb mixed ham and chicken
2 oz flour	4 small red skinned apples
1 pt milk	grated rind of lemon
1 egg	breadcrumbs.

Chop meat finely or put through mincer. Chop apples with skin after coring. Melt margarine in the milk and stir in the flour. Stir rapidly without cooking until mixture forms into a ball in the centre of the pan. Add chopped meats, apple and lemon rind. Allow to cool. Form into rolls and coat with egg and breadcrumbs. Place on flat tray so they do not touch and put trays into polythene bags to freeze. Remove trays when frozen and return croquettes to bag.

To Serve.

Deep fry croquettes until golden brown from frozen. Drain on kitchen paper and serve with salad. Or fry in a shallow fat turning constantly to brown all over. Can be served with rice. Allow 2 oz rice per person. Boil in plenty of salted water for approximately 15 min. Drain into a colander and rinse with hot water to separate grains. A combination of other left-over meats could replace chicken.

Storage time 2 months.   **Freezer space $\frac{1}{8}$ cu ft.**

FISH CAKES

To make 16 cakes.

Ingredients.

2 tbs flour	1 tsp mustard
4 tbs milk	a little butter
vinegar	1 lb cooked potatoes
4 tbs fish stock	1 lb cooked fish
cornflour	1 egg.
breadcrumbs	

Make a white sauce with the milk and fish stock thickened with cornflour. Season and add mustard. Beat in a knob of butter and a few drops of vinegar. Allow to cool, mash the potatoes, and mix in the fish and some chopped parsley if liked. Bind with the sauce and season to taste. Shape into 16 cakes on a floured board and dip in beaten egg and coat in breadcrumbs. Freeze on flat trays not allowing the cakes to touch. Place trays in polythene bags. Remove trays when frozen and return cakes to bags.

To Serve.

Fry fish cakes in deep fat until golden brown. Or fry in shallow fat turning to brown both sides. Garnish with parsley and lemon slices and serve with chipped potatoes and green vegetables. Most varieties of fish make tasty cakes but the addition of some proprietary fish paste gives more flavour and an interesting colour. Grated cheese, too, could be added with good effect.

Storage time 2 months.   **Freezer space $\frac{1}{8}$ cu ft.**

RISSOLES

To make 10 rissoles.

Ingredients.

1 lb mashed potatoes	½ tsp garlic salt (optional)
6 oz minced, cooked meat	1 egg
1 tbs tomato purée	1 onion.

Most cooked meats are satisfactory for this recipe but beef gives a stronger flavour. The Savoury Mince recipe is ideal. Mince the onion finely and mix into the meat and potatoes. Add the purée and garlic salt and bind with the egg. Form into round flat cakes on a floured board and put to freeze on flat trays not touching. Place trays in large polythene bags. Trays can be removed when rissoles are frozen and the rissoles stored in the bags. If preferred, the cakes can be dipped in beaten egg and then breadcrumbs.

To Serve.
Fry until golden brown in hot shallow fat turning to brown both sides. Serve with salad or green vegetables.

POTATO CROQUETTES

Mashed potatoes can be frozen and stored in polythene bags to be reheated in a greased casserole in warm oven. But if formed into croquettes and dipped in beaten egg and breadcrumbs they can be deep fried when required. Serve with cold meats and salad or in place of creamed potatoes.

Storage time 3 months.   **Freezer space minimal.**

SAUSAGE MEAT BALLS

To make approximately 16 balls.

Ingredients.

I small onion	8 oz pork sausage meat
½ oz margarine	1 oz breadcrumbs
2 chicken livers	seasoning.

Chop onion and fry until soft but not brown. Remove from pan and fry chicken liver in same fat to brown. Put the liver through a fine mincer and mix with sausage meat and breadcrumbs. Add the onion and the fat used for frying. Season to taste and mix well. Roll into balls on a floured board, about 16. Roll in flour or breadcrumbs. Freeze on trays so they do not touch. When frozen, pack into polythene bags. When chickens are bought in bulk it is a good plan to make the accompanying stuffings, etc. Then when a bird is roasted all the trimmings are available without further work.

To Serve.
Cook from frozen in the fat round the bird for the last hour, turning to brown.

Storage time 3 months.   **Freezer space minimal.**

SIMPLE SAGE AND ONION STUFFING

Chop and boil until tender 2 lb onions. Season and stir in a packet of sage and onion mix. Colour with gravy-browning. Freeze in waxed cartons for maximum 3 months.

MUSHROOM STUFFING

To make 8 oz stuffing.

Ingredients.

4 oz mushrooms	1 oz margarine
1 shallot	2 oz breadcrumbs
1 tbs parsley	1 egg
	seasoning.

Chop mushrooms and shallot and fry in margarine for 5 min. Leave until cold. Add parsley, seasoning and breadcrumbs to cold mixture and bind with beaten egg. Put into waxed containers and freeze.

To Serve.
Allow to thaw and use to stuff large vegetables such as marrow. Or stuff tomatoes or peppers. Bake vegetables in moderate oven according to size and type.

CELERY STUFFING

To make 10 oz stuffing.

Ingredients.

4 oz cooked celery	1 tbs parsley
4 oz breadcrumbs	seasoning
2 oz suet	beaten egg.
rind of ½ a lemon	

Chop celery and mix with breadcrumbs, suet and grated rind of lemon. Add parsley and seasoning. Bind with beaten egg and milk if necessary. Freeze in waxed containers.

To Serve.
Put in casserole with white fish and bake dotted with butter.

Storage time 3 months.   **Freezer space minimal.**

FORCEMEAT STUFFING

To make ½ lb stuffing.

Ingredients.

4 oz breadcrumbs	2 tsp parsley
2 oz suet	rind of ½ lemon
1-2 oz bacon or ham	¼ tsp mixed herbs.
1 egg	

Chop the bacon or ham, mix with breadcrumbs, herbs, suet and parsley. Grate in the lemon rind. Mix with a little beaten egg to bind. Shape balls on a floured board. Put on to trays not touching, to freeze. Store in polythene bags when frozen.

To Serve.

Fry in deep fat or cook round the fowl or joint until brown.

CHESTNUT STUFFING

To make sufficient for 1 fowl.

Ingredients.

1 lb chestnuts	1 tsp parsley
½ pt stock	lemon rind grated
2 oz ham or bacon, minced	sugar to taste
3-4 oz breadcrumbs	1 egg.

Slit ends of nuts and boil for 10 min. Shell. Simmer in stock until tender and mash. Add breadcrumbs ham and parsley, sugar, lemon rind and bind with egg. Freeze in waxed containers. Stuff fowl before roasting.

Storage time 4 months.   **Freezer space ⅛ cu ft.**

POTTED MEAT

To make 5-6 portions.

Ingredients.

8 oz cooked meat	seasoning
4 oz bacon	1 tbs tomato ketchup
1 small onion	1 egg.
2 oz breadcrumbs	

Put meat and onion through fine mincer or electric blender. Mix with breadcrumbs, ketchup and seasoning. Bind with the egg and press into a foil- lined basin or loaf-tin. Steam in a large pan for 1 hr. Allow sufficient time to cool and put potted meat into polythene bag to freeze. Container may be removed when completely frozen. Savoury Mince can be used in this recipe but omit onion and ketchup. It may be found necessary to increase the amount of breadcrumbs. Minced chicken and cowheel well seasoned and steamed as above makes a splendid potted meat also. Or the chicken and cowheel can be simmered together in a very little water and then turned into a foillined container to set before freezing.

To Serve.

Allow all potted meats to thaw to room temperature. Use as a sandwich filling or serve sliced with salad.

Storage time 3 months.   **Freezer space $\frac{1}{8}$ cu ft.**

PORK LIVER PATE

To make one and a half pounds of liver pâté.

Ingredients.

oil for frying

4 oz streaky bacon

4 oz pigs' liver

8 oz cooked pork

1 onion

4 oz belly pork

4 oz breadcrumbs

1 tsp black pepper

1 tsp rosemary

1 egg

stock.

Brown the liver in a little oil and put through a fine mincer or blender, with the pork, bacon and belly pork and the onion. Mix in the breadcrumbs and the pepper and rosemary. Do not add salt as the belly pork is salty. Bind the mixture with the egg and a little stock to achieve a dropping consistency. Line two loaf tins with foil and press the mixture into them. Cover with greaseproof paper and bake in a moderate oven for 2-2½ hr at 350° Reg 4. Allow sufficient time for pâté to cool completely and either freeze in the tins placed in polythene bags or cut into portions and freeze wrapped in foil.

To Serve.

Allow pâté to thaw to room temperature and serve with savoury biscuits and salad. The pâté may also be served with crisp toast as a starter before dinner. Use also as a sandwich filling as it is much more tasty than cooked cold meats.

Storage time 1 month.   **Freezer space minimal.**

CHICKEN LIVER PATE

To make 1 lb of pâté.

Ingredients.

giblets of three chickens
   including necks
3 oz breadcrumbs
2 tbs sage and onion mix
2 oz bacon

4 oz sausage meat
1 egg
1 onion
seasoning.

Simmer the giblets in a little water until tender. Remove unwanted skin and pick the meat from the necks. Put the meat, bacon, giblets and onion through a fine mincer or electric blender. Mix in the sausage meat and bread-crumbs. Season to taste. Stir in the sage and onion and blend all together with the egg. Add a little of the giblet stock if mixture too dry. Line a loaf tin with foil allowing the foil to protrude over the rim and press the mixture into the tin. Cover with greaseproof paper and bake in hot oven 400° Reg 6 for 1 hr or until firm. Allow to cool in tin and freeze whole or in portions as required. The tin can be removed when pâté is frozen.

To Serve.
Allow pâté to thaw to room temperature and serve with savoury biscuits and salad. Or use as a sandwich filling.

Storage time 1 month.   **Freezer space minimal.**

LIVER PATE

To make 1 lb of liver pâté.

Ingredients.

oil for frying
1 onion
8 oz liver
2 oz bacon
4 oz sausage meat

2 oz breadcrumbs
1 egg
½ tsp garlic salt
seasoning.

Chop the onion and brown in a little oil. Fry the liver. Mince the liver, onion, bacon and breadcrumbs together. Mix in the sausage meat. Add the garlic salt and any other seasoning preferred. Bind together with the egg and a little stock if too dry. Line a loaf tin with foil allowing the foil to protrude over the rim of the tin. Press the mixture into the tin and cover loosely with greaseproof paper. Bake in hot oven 400° Reg 6 for approximately 1 hr or until firm. Allow to cool in the tin and when cold put tin into a polythene bag and freeze. The tin may be removed on freezing. Alternatively, when completely cold, cut into portions and wrap in foil to freeze.

To Serve.
Allow to thaw to room temperature and serve with tiny savoury biscuits and salad.

Storage time 1 month.   **Freezer space minimal.**

INDEX

Index

160